The Hypnotic Wisdom of Telemarketing Success

Steve Ashman

About the Author

Steve Ashman is a Certified Hypnotherapist, Stage Hypnotist and Master Practitioner of Neuro Linguistic Programming and works in practise in Leicestershire, England. As a therapist he specialises solely in weight management and Hypno-Band, hypnotic gastric band surgery.

In addition to therapy, Steve tours with his show 'The Hypnotic Wisdom of Weight Loss', sharing his experience in the field of weight management and how hypnosis can be used to fascinating effect to improve many aspects of your life.

Having worked in sales for over twenty five years, Steve offers in this book a unique approach to Telemarketing discussing how to excel at the noble art of lead generation by refining your communication skills.

Steve is contactable through his web site at:

www.ashmanhypnosis.co.uk

Dedication

This work is dedicated to my wife, Marion Ashman for her love and support, to my friends and colleagues who work tirelessly in this industry and all of my clients that have benefited from hypnosis over the years.

Copyright

All rights reserved.
Copyright © Steve Ashman 2014.

No part of this publication may be replicated, reproduced or transmitted in any form without the express written permission of the copyright owner and publisher.

This book is sold on the proviso that it will not be lent, re-sold or hired out or circulated in any form without the publisher's written prior permission. The original purchaser may save a single copy of the e-book and print a single copy, for personal use only.

All rights reserved.

Table of Contents
The Benefits of Effective Telemarketing
The Secrets of Successful Telemarketing
Creating a compelling unique business presentation
Up-front Preparation
Summary – The Professional World of Telemarketing

The Benefits of Effective Telemarketing
What is telemarketing?

Telemarketing is a collective term which encompasses the procedures successful sales people use to widen their appeal to greater audiences using the telephone as a tool. The art of effective telemarketing is a learned skill that requires a set of clear objectives, proven techniques and purposeful refinement in an aid to gain successful exposure in your chosen market.

A dynamic and successful telemarketing person is the key to growth in any business, forging new relationships which otherwise would fail to materialise. You may have already found that many forms of marketing are speculative in their arrangements. Having already spent money on all manner of marketing such as advertising, web sites and direct mail for promises of new leads, you may have already realised that the return on your investment had not always lived up to your expectation or that the results were un-measurable at best.

The Hypnotic Wisdom of Telemarketing Success is here to break away the myths about using the telephone in sales and open your eyes to real, measurable gains. You will no longer have to rely on your gut feel and the opinions of an army of employees and sales people to make the choice that is right for you. Right here you'll gain an understanding of how the telemarketing process works, whether you are a one-man-business, new to the world of sales or whether you want to better equip your existing sales force.

You may be reading this with the thought that telesales people are an immoral element of society that exist to pester, cajole and alleviate the weak into parting with their hard earned savings, producing crooked transactions that are irretraceable in the world of commerce. Well I am here to tell you it is not. Telemarketing is a worthwhile and needed part of industry. Granted, as with any sales or business technique that is available to the masses, it can be used as an unscrupulous tool, tainting the hard work of the legitimate. In the main, telemarketing is honourable and a worthy profession generating large sums of incomes for its operators and employers.

Why should you consider telemarketing?
You know, marketing managers feel the need to change their approach with each new development or fad that comes along. From a web presence, to social media, to e-marketing, each one of these new ideas eating into the resources of the company in both time and finances, but telemarketing remains the number one method of lead generation today.

Why is that?

Because it works! Think about it, talking to someone on the phone is the next best thing to face to face meetings. The communication a trained and responsive telemarketer generates is guided and driven by the response they hear. This is one of the presuppositions or principles of NLP – Neuro Linguistic Programming, the meaning of the communication you make is the response that you get. In a face to face conversation with someone you may ask a question and choose the direction of the conversation based on the answer you get from the person in front of you, telemarketing is no different. When you are face-to-face with a person the dominant sense is sight. Your brain picks up thousands of tiny movements and interprets them. It is easy to decide if a person is attentive and interested, if you can see their body language.

By fine tuning your abilities on the phone you will reduce the amount of time you spend with the wrong sort of clients, by only pursuing those that have the requirement and intention to make a purchase. In this book we'll be looking at how to identify your requirement criteria and how to qualify prospects intentions. As you aim to hit the heights of the top sales achievers in the world today, you will want to focus on the right type of deal and reduce the amount of time you spend.

Even though telemarketing is the most effective form of lead generation you will want to take advantage of other mediums that create a collaborative effect on your success. The data you work will move from a state of unusable stagnancy, to highly profitable, due to the actions of your calls and your subsequent efforts to update the database. An active contact database will yield more new clients with each day that passes, the success of emailing campaigns will rise and further follow ups will result in increased business.

A carefully planned telemarketing strategy is not a speculative undertaking. There are costs and time involved as with all methods of lead generation, but this way is measured and reliable. On a day to day basis the method shown in this book will show you how to predict the amount of business you will generate, all you have to do is follow this training.

Why is telemarketing so effective?
With direct speech you know where you stand, it isn't hearsay or hyperbole. It is simply a communication between two people. In telemarketing we are looking for a middle ground where the conversation feels comfortable and can possibly flourish.

But, telemarketing is about manipulating the host to get our own way?

No, it isn't. There are companies out there that try to trap you with each question and force your decision making down a route you don't want to go. Manipulating your prospect will leave them feeling cheated. Why would you want to do that? Your organisation is a credible and honest business that has developed an outstanding reputation over the years, now is not the time to put that into jeopardy.

A highly motivated telemarketer that can create leads for your business will end up becoming ideal candidates for promotion into the account management and new business arena for you. There are no associated costs with recruiting them into this part of the business and you can attest to their future success with historical measurements you've recorded in their time in telesales.

As part of the sales team function, telemarketers are paid in the majority on results. They make good margin for themselves and for your business and stay loyal to the process. The more business they do, the more the business grows and the more they get paid, there is no greater influence on focus.

What's hypnotic about telemarketing?
Hypnosis and NLP – Neuro Linguistic Programming are art forms that rely on interpreting body language and conscious and unconscious communication to affect change and influence people. Telemarketing is exactly the same principle. The telemarketer needs to read the signals received in the conversation before quickly translating the response and guiding the prospect in the desired ethical direction.

In most conversations these signals happen automatically, but by understanding what they are the telemarketer can pre-empt and adapt their approach to change the outcome. A person's reason to buy a product/service or come on board with one of your ideas is strongly affected by emotion. Does your prospect feel comfortable with you? Are they convinced that this is the right decision or will they suffer buyer's remorse? When is the right time to continue or more importantly stop the conversation?

The restrictive cost of conventional marketing
When you market your company, its products and services, invariably cost is the most important consideration. The money leaves your bank account and from that moment on you are looking for a return on your investment. For instance, if you take space at an exhibition, the resulting leads may take days, weeks or months to come to fruition, if at all. So how do you really measure success?

One sale might be all it takes to make any event or advertising worthwhile. The Hypnotic Wisdom of Telemarketing Success will teach you not only how to plan, but how to record information to ensure you can account for your actions and guarantee success. You'll know exactly what you've spent, exactly what it takes to generate a sale and what you have to do right now to continue.

You won't have to 'speculate to accumulate' any longer. Our roadmap is clear and will let you transfer your success into other members of the team by simply following the same process. If you know where you are and where you want to be, then this book will give you the rest.

Why do so many people have trouble with telemarketing?
Having worked in sales for over twenty five years, I've met so many great sales people that have an outright aversion to making calls and speaking to people. My colleagues have been excellent examples of the sales art, excelling in all areas of the profession including strategic planning, presentations, negotiation, etc except they seem to fall apart when it comes to picking up the phone.

They say that 95% of people would rather die than give a presentation. Well, telemarketing seems to have the same stigma. Why is telemarketing so different from a conversation in a prospects office? Why does the thought of picking up the phone instil an uncontrollable fear?

It's hard to imagine. Everyone I know spends their entire time on their mobile phones talking to their friends and customers, but that positive aura seems to die with prospects. Perhaps it's the thought of rejection or the prospect saying no or maybe the rudeness that some people exude that ignites even higher levels of depression in the caller.

All of these things are limiting beliefs, an internal system that is holding you back. There is no rationality behind these beliefs. Contrary to popular belief, an unhappy or angry prospect cannot climb through the handset and intimidate you. Someone saying no to you is not a personal slur on your character. In fact, a no, doesn't make any difference to you at all.

These irrational fears are exactly the same as other fears in life. A fear of all dogs, maybe because you were bitten as a child is a good example. A person may have an irrational fear of heights even though the structure that they are standing on is perfectly safe.

These fears are so strong that even when we decide to sit and do these calls because we are convinced that telemarketing will help us, we procrastinate. We prioritise other work and convince our colleagues and managers that we had more imperative and important things to do first. We surf the internet and find a million other things to do and we simply do not make the calls.

It's no wonder then, that the word gets around that telemarketing doesn't work. The truth is, telemarketing is a highly responsive and successful way to bring new business into any organisation, but you have to do it. In later chapters, we'll look at the real traits of a successful person and give you the tools to succeed.

In this book we'll show you
We'll be looking at the secrets of successful telemarketing. How you develop the traits of a successful telemarketer and dispel the myths that hold all the others back. We're including the methods used to plan and record your actions along with how to predict your future pipeline.

We'll explore how successful telemarketers create a unique and compelling message about the product or service they supply that satisfies the need of the prospect. With these techniques you have the ability to deliver information that opens the door leaving your new contact wanting more.

The Hypnotic Wisdom of Telemarketing Success opens its bag of techniques and delivers a step-by-step explanation and scenarios that allow you to learn at your own pace. Each technique will blend professionally with your current knowledge, increasing your opportunity to close. We'll be looking at identifying the phases of the call and how a perfectly timed response will broaden your prospects expectation.

We'll be looking at amalgamating your new found knowledge and improving your confidence in the calling process. You'll discover how professional telemarketers review their own working patterns and accelerate success.

The Secrets of Successful Telemarketing
What are the traits of a successful telemarketing professional?

Having reached chapter two of this book, you have already begun the journey. Generous helpings of curiosity and determination will have got you this far. By making the decision that you want to learn more, in hypnosis terms this is called creating an up-time trance, you have broadened your horizons in anticipation of information. If we don't create an open and positive emotional state and appropriate environment for learning, no amount of useful training will have any sort of desired effect. Think about it, have you ever tried to teach an uninterested teenager something important and they don't want to listen. The words 'so what' spring to mind, only to find that they absorb every piece of data when they find a subject that really inspires them? Quite often the only difference between the two situations is that you find out that one of their close friends has been involved in some sort of recommendation, a method of profound influence.

The creation of a positive emotional state and a deep desire to learn is all it takes to fire up the brains synapses and the information will flow into the subconscious. From that moment on, everything we have learned becomes useful. With perfect practice, comes perfection. Yes I mean perfect practise. If you practise imperfection it will become the norm, take your time and learn each step properly. Follow the steps in each chapter and you simply won't go wrong.

A good telemarketer develops an unending tenacity and unwavering positive nature. Most people think that picking the phone up all day long is tough, but it simply isn't. In most jobs in the sales arena, whether its account management, on site demonstrating or negotiating a close, stress is often an irritating side effect. A professional telemarketer creates a working environment that is separated from everything that can distract or affect their progress. When you make the calls, you are making them on your terms. The conversations that you have are always under your control. You may grade each telephone call based on the quality of your success and how emotional it made you feel, but that is it. A telemarketer is not fazed by the ups and downs that occur throughout the day, in fact, a poor quality interaction will offer an opportunity to change approach and refine technique. Do you think that a professional telemarketer is disturbed by the occasional rude prospect? Of course not, bear in mind that perfectly normal and reasonable people have bad days and you may have just called them at the wrong time.

Always be courteous and polite, no matter what happens. Keep the call short and get off the phone. Don't let someone else's bad mood affect your outlook and motivation.

In telemarketing be studious, organised and always do what you say you are going to do. When you get under the bonnet of this role you will need to keep exceptional records about the interactions and conversations you have with people. You can of course, adopt software to help you in this area, but remember the software and its diarised reminders are only as good as your intention to action them. Prospects may not always have the time to speak to you with every call you make, but at least it shows your reliability and efficiency as positive traits.

Busting the myths we all believe
The first myth is that telemarketers just read scripts. Like robots they learn a routine and stick to it with dog eared determination. The conversation may veer uncontrollably at times, but the script drags the conversation back on course, hypnotising and influencing the unsuspecting prospect.

Let me clarify this, telemarketers that use scripts badly are easily identifiable. They don't listen. Their inner thoughts are more focussed onto what happens next, that they miss the golden nuggets of information that can make all the difference in the outcome of the call. If you sound like you are reading words off a sheet, the prospect will instantly know they are being sold to and the chances of proceeding any further are limited at best.   Lesson number one is, this is an interaction, a conversation between two people, not a one sided information gathering exercise. Endless reams of questioning do little to get any one on board.

Notice I didn't say scripts are bad, they are not. Scripts are a means to develop best practise. By writing down the words and importantly, practising them out loud, you can create a powerful vocabulary that will set you apart from other sales people. This is the art of self assessment, listening to your performance and demanding more from your talent.

You may have heard some of the great speeches of the famous and infamous in history, delivered as if an ad-hoc display of verbal dexterity. Well you'd be wrong. Behind great orators are great writers that refine the art of getting their words to have the greatest impact. The impact is in the delivery. Not just a seemingly endless list of words, but a compelling vision delivered with impeccable timing. A great speaker listens thoughtfully and with empathy and uses effective body language to gain trust. A telemarketer does exactly the same thing. Only in their world they replace the visual clues with auditory equivalents.

When you prepare, feel free to write your ideas down in a book, all of them count. Use the book to record your progress, see how far you come in such a short space of time. Marvel at words and sentences that when written down work beautifully, yet when spoken out loud seem to lose the chosen effect.

The written word is a planning tool and planning is the number one activity that will guarantee you success. Getting on the phone and winging it will almost certainly lead to poor quality results in the long term.

How many times have you heard the phrase 'it's a numbers game', or 'the more you call, the more you'll close?'   Keeping your number of calls up is important, but calling for calling sake won't bring you the results you desire. We'll take a look at the difference between cold and warm market and the vast difference in results. It is vitally important to set yourself both a financial and activity target to exceed with each session. Every sales person must know their numbers if they intend succeed on any level. Do you know the answer to:

- What is your average sale value?

- How many new sales do you need to make this month?

- How many calls do you have to make to sell an appointment?

- How many appointments turn into a sale?

There are many more questions and the answers are all numbers. A good sales manager can spot a winner in the sales department, if they have a plan and can easily display a working knowledge of sales ratios and business planning. Later we will cover this in greater detail. You don't have to be a mathematical genius or an accountant to make numbers work for you. Keep them simple.

Shutting the world out and getting focussed

Distraction and procrastination is the sales person's greatest enemy. In a role that is mainly office based the telemarketer is at the mercy of all manner of disturbance. The favourites to avoid are the office banter or gossip merchants that want to draw you into a prolonged and inane discussion to simply waste time.   Office colleagues that don't have to account for their time, or have no sales target, do not have to account for their role with numbers on the board, you do! The answer to keep them from disturbing you is having the telephone handset in your hand at all times. It's amazing how many telemarketers make excuses by saying I didn't have time today because the incoming calls were excessive. If you are on the phone you don't have to answer those calls. Make it someone else's priority, not yours.

Look around, how many of your colleagues come in to the office at 9am and make a drink, wasting the first twenty minutes. Some even slouch in later and eat breakfast wasting even more time. It doesn't sound much does it, but that's the equivalent of seven hours lost a month. Plan the night the before and get in ten minutes early each morning, make yourself a coffee and hit the phone as they walk in, they can't disturb you. In fact, if you play your cards right, you might even be included in the tea round again.

Beware the time thief, the wanderer, the person without portfolio that aimlessly attempts to stop everyone else from working. This is the someone that pulls you into a meeting for no reason, pulls up a chair to discuss last nights TV and generally stalls your efforts to be successful. What do you want the most, to be the most personable and friendly person in the office or the most profitable and successful?

Set your stall out for success. If you hit the phone at 9am, by 10am you can already have ten calls in the bag. Twenty calls by 11am and so on. As you knock off for a well earned lunch at 1pm you will have made more calls than most of your sales colleagues collectively. Hitting the magic numbers of forty, fifty or sixty calls by the halfway point of the day means that you are well on the way to a measured and financially profitable success. Be visible, post your figures in a place where everyone can see them. Use the motivation that this brings to constantly exceed your own targets and stay ahead of others. It won't be long before your efforts come to fruition and you are financially recognised.

High call numbers are not the only element of success, but you have to make calls and as you'll discover knowing how many calls you need for success means that you will prioritise your day accordingly.

Less calls, more success

In my early career as a salesman, marketing was somewhat different than it is today. With no internet, we relied heavily on direct mail followed by telemarketing to gauge interest. My manager would divide the local Yellow Pages between the sales-force and ask us to ring each entry in turn. (Don't do this now) Granted our products were ideal for the home market and back in the eighties there seemed to be an unending supply of leads that came from this method. Home owners seemed to relish the fact that we had something new, something interesting to tell them about, but the internet has changed all that.

Nowadays, if you were to call any directory list this would be known as cold calling. This type of approach is attacking data that is stone cold, has had no contact from you before and you have no idea if they have a need for your product or service. I did say, this is a numbers game though and if you hit the phones hard enough you will undoubtedly uncover an opportunity at some point by ringing from a list. Believe me, its hard graft, lots and lots of calls and a various range of rewards.

Any sales person that has joined a company and been involved with this type of calling may now be scarred for life and understandably will appear less than willing to fall headlong into such heartache.   No-one likes to do a lot, for a little, it isn't the way we are programmed. Working hard has its merits, but working smarter is far more appealing.

How do you make your life easier and warm the market?

Let's take a step back. Success breads success. Prospects want to buy from businesses that are doing well and the best type of warm lead is a referral. Every time you do business with someone ask them for a referral.

"I can see that you are happy with the work we've done, do you know anyone else that would be interested in what we do?"

How easy is it to phone a referral on the back of your conversation with a customer and mention their name? In most cases, the prospect will give you the time of day and at least listen to what you have to offer.   Get in the habit of asking the question when you've done something good for someone. It doesn't have to be a customer. It can be anyone that you have helped. If you have done a good deed, been asked for advice or even discussed business with a passer by, be nonchalant and ask:

"Our business is specialist in double glazing and conservatories, do you know any friends or family that you think could do with new windows?"

"Our business specialises in hire machinery for the building trade, can you think of anyone that would benefit from these services?"

There are myriads of ways to ask for referrals, so follow these steps to make them effective.

1. Write a phrase you are happy with and practise it out loud.

2. Use the phrase in as many conversations as you can.

3. Make a note of the referral and add it to your warm market list.

I've included a few variations of the phrase below within particular industry contexts. You will need to adjust these to be more specific. Remember that the written word and the spoken word are two entirely different things. When you write down a phrase and read it, you are simply internalising the words making sense of the structure. When you read the phrase out loud your ears create additional meaning and add congruency to the message. Some sentences won't work because they're too long or words are too awkward to say or don't fit in the context of your approach.

You have an in-built convincer strategy that tells you when you are comfortable with your phrase. Repetition is the mother of all learning, literally. Repeat the phrase out loud, over and over. You may want to find a quiet place to do this, or you may receive funny looks from passers-by. The way you phrase the question will change with practise. All you are aiming to do is deliver the question in a way that tells the prospect that you ask the question of everyone and importantly, get a result every time.

Try some of these:

"How many other finance directors do you know that are looking at the spiralling costs of paper?"

"You're a member of the Federation of Small Businesses right, do you ever discuss financing?

"I'm looking to offer a greater number of people cheaper restaurant meals in this area, can you recommend anyone I can talk to?"

Referrals may look old fashioned in this world of social media, texts and emailing, but it doesn't hurt your standing in the eyes of the customer to be looking to do even more. If you've done a great job and the customer likes what you've done, won't they want to tell their friends?

A professional business person will want to create a collection of case studies in each vertical market that they operate. In a simple PDF format or printed sheet, the case study is additional proof that you can supply a quality product or service in a similar way, to a similar business. What is more comforting to a new contact than this sort of proof?

Anyway, back on track. Warm market leads are easier to sell to, so how do we generate more? Use a collaborative approach. Telemarketing on its own is possible and does work, but what if you use additional marketing to contact your cold data first. First of all let's go back to the beginning.

In the 1980's marketing professionals would 'speculate to accumulate' spending time and money on advertising, direct mail, exhibitions and face-to-face meetings. It was hard to see the return on investment that was gained by using each method, all we hoped was that some new business would come of it to cover the costs.

Nowadays, all the marketing we do is highly critical of expenditure and adds in a measured way to the collaborative approach. For instance, we may buy data for a particular vertical market containing email addresses from a credible source. We would email that data with a relevant message recording the number of people that not only opened the email, but visited our web site as a result. These interests would form the basis of our warm market possibilities.

There is a sliding scale of opportunity here from the 'I've heard of your company, but have no need to buy' to the 'I am seriously interested in the product and would like more information'. There is a cost to the data, lets face it if you were to source the data manually from directory lists or advertising, clean it, adding the right name of the decision maker and ring to capture the email addresses it would be a costly exercise. Buying it may be the cheaper option. Email software packages with the ability to produce click and open reports are readily available on the internet. A click and open report shows you the interest of those you have emailed by indicating which of them actually opened the email and clicked through to specific places on the web site. These are tools that are measurable and can greatly increase your level of success.

Attack a target market that's right for you

Depending on your product or service, there may be more than one market that would welcome you, due diligence and research at the start of your business will save you a lot of time later on. The question is a simple one, is their sufficient population to sell my product or service to?

There is no point making hundreds of phone calls if you come to the conclusion that no-one wants or needs your product. We may see that selling ice cream to Alaskans or bags of sand to tribes in the Gobi desert is funny, but is it a similar picture in our market place.

Be clear in your mind.

- Can you market to an international, national and local audience?

- Is the price point of your offering within the realms of possibility for your audience?

- Does your offering solve a particular need or could it be perceived as a must have item?

- What is the quantity of product that you need to move to achieve profitability?

- Do you know the detail of your prospects requirement?

- If you are selling to companies, which particular person do you want to speak to? (Finance directors, sales people, managers, etc)

These questions can easily be overlooked, but this is a mistake. Take advice, ask around, do market research, search the internet and most importantly of all do a test number of calls and be critical of your approach and results. If you make 100 calls you are well on the way to understanding the results you will gain overall.

There is a highly effective process that can be used to clearly identify if the prospects you are talking to are worthwhile and will bring the results you want. The acronym **SCOTSMAN** contains all of the components for qualification and will work in the majority of industries.

S	Solution
C	Competition
O	Only Me
T	Timescale
S	Size
M	Money
A	Authority
N	Need

Solution. The prospect will only consider your product or service based on one of three things. Either the offering will satisfy a direct need or requirement in the business, an indirect need or there will be a desire to own the item which falls in the area of an emotional purchase.

Direct need. Supplying a product to fulfil a need has a simple logic. Say for instance, a prospect needs to make their house more secure due to a recent burglary and your company offers a lock to replace the one broken in the burglary. Hey presto! You have matched the need and with the price agreed the transaction can take place. The prospect knew what they wanted and you met their need.

Indirect need. The sale can take a broader scope. In the case of a burglary you may gain interest based on their need, but during the sales call you may offer the possibility of a product or service that indirectly impacts on the emotion of the prospect. They may be looking for a new lock, but the sale may also represent additional insurance, closed circuit television cameras or other items of security. The effect of emotion in a traumatic situation such as theft or a burglary will understandably increase the level of persuasion in the sale. This is not to say that a prospect should be taken advantage of in their hour of need, this is to state that we all buy with some element of emotion. If the sales person cannot change the emotional state of the prospect then the sale will never take place.

Desire to own. Some products in life sell in large numbers for no sensible reason other than the prospect has some reference point. It may be a hobby that grasps their imagination, or a product that a peer group all own or a supply and demand situation exists, where the product has known scarcity. In selling in general, if you are desperate to make a sale, the prospect picks up on the unconscious signals in your communication and will often interpret them in a negative way and eventually your sales pipeline dries up. Scarcity has the opposite effect, it creates a market place and here lies our return to referrals. Can you cite users of your products? Does a famous person in the industry endorse what you do? Why is it that the best products in life don't necessarily turn out to be the best sellers?

To give yourself a tick in the box for **Solution,** answer the following truthfully?

- For this client do I have a solution for their direct need? (chunked down – do you have the detail of the need?)

- Do I have an offering that would benefit the wider requirement? (chunked up – can you identify additional scope?)

- Is my solution, a wanted, an in demand or desired piece that will sell itself?

The term chunked, comes from the works of the great motivational speaker Tony Robbins and is a way of describing how a conversation can benefit from probing at the detail (chunked down) or expanding the thoughts of the person by looking at the global picture (chunking up). We will use this methodology later in the book when we look at the process of influence and objection handling.

Competition. It is unusual in life to not have any competition whatsoever and when a sales person makes this claim about a sales opportunity I am always sceptical. Why? With the help of the internet we are in a global market and at least one other company in the world will be doing exactly the same as you, I can guarantee it. Hundreds of others will have solutions that overlap in some way and yet more will have small elements that will satisfy part of the need and may catch the eye of the prospect.

In competition terms you have two other concerns. There may be an incumbent supplier who the prospect has a working knowledge of and the prospect may do nothing at all. Imagine this from the prospects point of view, it may be less hassle and less of a worry after all the sales meetings and phone calls you make to sit exactly where they are and do nothing, its human nature. The fear that it may all go wrong, cost them money and time or their boss pointing and blaming them. In the same way, if the emotion to drive the project is replaced by procrastination you may face the unhappy situation that your prospect stands still rather than buys from you.

To give yourself a tick in the box for **Competition,** answer the following truthfully?

- Have I asked the prospect if they are considering any other product or service in this regard? (It is vitally important to know your product well and an added bonus to understand competitive products and their failings)

- Do you know who the current supplier of the product is and why would this prospect consider moving away? (Keep your ears open for any inference that the supplier is less than capable)

- Do you have at least one reason why the prospect will not delay? (a compelling event)

Compelling events are the best way to gain commitment. If the prospects insurance expires in two weeks time, then you have a need and an emotional desire to successfully close that sale without delay. Open ended requirements are always at risk of the prospect delaying the purchase.

Only me. In the next chapter we are going to be looking at creating a compelling business case that defines an array of positive messages and business arguments that drive your prospect emotionally towards the sale. The business value proposition or unique selling points of your product are created in a clear context to allow your offering to sit head and shoulders above any other proposition they are considering.

You can only do this if you understand who the competition really are. A business argument you deliver might look really weak if you are pitching against other products or services of which you have no former knowledge. You cannot be precise unless you have been honest with yourself in regards to the competition. If you haven't asked the client who you are up against then you have created a situation that leaves you on a back foot from the word go.

To give yourself a tick in the box for **Only Me,** answer the following truthfully?

- Do I fully appreciate how the competition is viewed by my prospect?

- What do my competitors have as unique selling points and what strong points will my pitch need to emphasise?

Timescale. When you understand the determining factors behind the prospects decision making process you can move forward. There is no point offering a special offer price if they are not willing to conduct the transaction now. Timescale is at the heart of all sales processes. It is your role as the telemarketer to find that reason, that compelling event that is going to shorten the sales cycle.

If they don't have a compelling event, then why are they looking at your product now? Window shoppers or tyre kicker's use up your valuable time and become an administrative burden in your database and pipeline. We'll discuss the pipeline process later on, but at the moment we'll stay with the important aspect of why not now?

In the individual stages of the sales cycle you make contact, conduct a needs analysis questioning, qualify the deal and negotiate to close. By missing the qualification phase you are opening the door to sales that are always on the cusp, but never close and become business. When you make initial contact you are importantly building rapport, at this stage the prospect will already know if your company is worth dealing with. In the questioning phase, you are building a picture of the requirement, eventually matching that need to the product or service that you offer. That's why it's best not to sell too early until you know all the facts. Now, qualification is where timescale fits in to all this. You must ask:

- When do you need to go live on this project?
- How quickly do you need this?
- What's your deadline for having this up and running?
- What more do you have to do before you place the order?

Can you see where these questions are leading you? Imagine the following answers:

- I'm just interested in the product, I don't need to do anything this year
- I'm in no rush, when is it cheapest?

- I have another ten suppliers to see who is going to give me the best deal

On the phone call you know where you stand. You won't be qualifying them or spending lots of time chasing them up for an order and you would certainly fall flat on your face if you attempted to close at this point. On the other hand if the answers are:

- I need to get the order placed this week as the move to the new office takes place on Tuesday

- No time like the present, I have more important things to do

- I have a couple of others to see and then I'll compare proposals

The art of closing on the phone is more to do with the build up and questioning than it is the ultimate closing question. If you hadn't asked about the timescale, it is easy to see that you would be suffering from a poor close ratio because some of those prospects have a legitimate reason to put off placing the order.

Size. Size is a reality check. It's a wake up call to walk before you can run. If as a telemarketer you get paid on the resulting sales of the appointments you've made, you'd have a vested interest in sending the right sales person to the right type of client wouldn't you? Then why pursue prospects that are either too large or too small for your organisation? This is often apparent when as a sales manager you discuss the pipeline with the telemarketer and you can see the extremes of size nestled in the list waiting to close. It is human nature to want to keep the biggest deals because one of those may help you instantly hit target. In reality, they are a distraction. They take up a whole lot more time and without the skills and capacity, delivery can be fraught with danger resulting in cash-flow issues.

It's really hard to see this at first, you want to make a good impression and chase it all, but in reality it may make you more money to lay off the larger deal to a competitor in exchange for a finder's fee and move on. Set an upper and lower limit that reflects your capabilities and commitment, nothing stops you from revising it later.

At this point, It would be useful to give you a range of questions that extract from the prospect all of their financial history, profit and losses and balance sheets. Of course, unless this information is registered at companies' house and in the public domain, you may find these questions are too intrusive and do little to build rapport.

- What is your turnover this year?

- What has been your profitability?

Both questions lack finesse. They have sharp edges that leave a bitter taste in the mouth and could easily offend. Be smart, use language softeners and play to their achievements:

- Where do you see the business in the next five years?

- How will you focus your attention over the next few years to grow the business?

Both of these questions, chunk up and ask the prospect to look at the bigger picture. As you are holding rapport with the prospect, complimenting them on their strategic abilities and taking an interest in their enterprising world, you are doing something really important. You are helping them to lower their critical thinking and develop an emotional thought, curiosity.

When you ask:

"Where do you see the business in the next five years?"

Most business owners will jump at the chance to explain their master plan to someone that is taking an interest. The resulting effect is the intention to share information and allow reciprocity to cultivate. The vision of the business is where your entire up-sell potential comes from. At least now you know if the size of this prospect is right for you.

Money. Did I not mention money? Probably the most important part of the sale, you getting paid. You simply can't ask:

"Do you have the money to pay for this?"

Again the words would upset even the hardest of temperaments. In certain contexts you could try:

- How do you normally finance IT purchases?

- Have you ever considered leasing as a way of spreading payments?

By asking these questions at the appropriate time, the prospect is likely to offer a wider view of their current opinion. Imagine the possible answers to the first question.

"We normally pay cash on delivery."

"The last one of these we purchased we were happy to use finance, its best for our business."

How long would you pursue a company or individual that was broke, leaving a trail of uncertainty in their wake? At what point do you stop and focus your attentions on other prospects? This is where your ability to question, listen empathetically and measure your responses is important. We are looking for an outcome that satisfies both parties. Do the answers you receive build a trustworthy and congruous picture?

Authority. When we speak to our prospects we begin to gauge a level of interest in the project. Some people will hold court by questioning at a skilled and technical level, whereas some prospects will undoubtedly want to understand the overall effect or potential for return on investment. There have been so many times in my career where I have failed to gain a full understanding of my prospects authority in the business and spent endless time supplying all manner of data and information for the lead to go dead.

The motivation and emotion you build in speaking with the prospect is lost in translation. This is to say that the words and techniques you use with your contact are rarely communicated in such a way to the decision maker in the business that they will make a positive decision in your favour. For example, you receive a call from a person who has seen your advertisement for energy saving light bulbs. In reality, they are 20% more expensive than the normal brand, but in the medium to long term the product, lasts longer and saves more. The person on the phone buys into your message and you ask for the order. If the person isn't the decision maker they may respond in the following way.

"I have to speak to my manager."

You say "OK, I'll call you in a couple of days."

From then on your contact is very difficult to get hold of. Every time you ring, they aren't in the office, or they are in a meeting, they don't answer your emails and all you get is excuses.

Read between the lines. Your brilliant sales pitch went inside their ears and got changed in translation. Firstly, the boss may have had no knowledge of the light bulbs and isn't interested in saving money, the company didn't have a real need. No need, no sale. Then his colleague, your contact has discussed his version of the product pitch with him. The boss isn't really interested and looks at one thing and one thing only the price. Stalemate, the original contact doesn't like to give bad news and your pipeline has continued to grow with all of the wrong type of prospects.

Get real. Stop wasting your time. Understanding the buying procedure in a business means that you need to talk to the person that can say yes, or no. Either way, you know where you stand. Most telemarketers are scared to ask the question. They are afraid of belittling or upsetting the contact and they are right to be concerned. Once again, soften your language.

- How does the company make decisions on purchases of this kind?
- Is there a purchasing procedure I need to be aware of?
- Can I ask about placing the order, will this be your decision?
- Are there any other people that would need to see the proposal before a decision is made?

All questions of this nature have to be delivered as part of a conversation. Just delivering them out of the blue will cause them to stick out boldly. Your prospect will expect you as a professional telemarketer to ask a series of questions after your product pitch has taken place, its called professionalism. In the same way, if you demonstrated a product to a person and didn't ask for the order, that would be odd, wouldn't it?

To give yourself a tick in the box for **Authority,** answer the following truthfully?

- Is this person in a position to say yes and sign off the finances?
- Do you know the names of all of the people that will be involved in the decision? (what is your strategy for speaking to them also)

Need. I was about to say, if you don't have a need you don't have a sale, although we do know that some things that sell are purchased on emotion alone. Status symbols, the Rolex watch, the iPad, the Ferrari car may all be purchased for the impact they have on the peer group of the purchaser. Nice to haves that you just buy to satisfy that urge. Cultivating brand at this level means you are doing something right, at the right time. In fairness, for the mere mortals of us, it is best to stick to one or two rules that help generate a greater demand and emotional need.

Always be upbeat about the thing you are selling. Your prospect will pick up on the finer points of negativity. Emphasise the positives and don't talk about the negatives. I'll say it again. Referrals and case studies that are meaningful to the prospect hold great credence in the sale.

Don't tell lies or tall tales about your product or service. These lies will always find you out. Be the trusted advisor and play the slightly longer game even if you have put your life savings into this new idea of yours and need to make money now. Bad news, not hitting deadlines and making promises that don't transpire are the quickest way to fail. Imagine you've had a bad meal at a restaurant, how many people do you tell about it? A lot. Nowadays with the internet, web sites are specifically designed to report about the failures of an establishment or experience and have a massive effect on a businesses success. Make sure all of the news about you is positive.

If you are promoting a solution based product find out what the need is before you offer a solution, don't assume anything. For instance, if you manufacture plastic potties for children, it would be reasonable to find out that the person you are speaking to is either a parent, a grandparent or wholesaler of baby items, wouldn't it?

Let's take that scenario a little further based on a news item I saw a few days ago. A young entrepreneur had designed a portable child's potty to solve the issue of using the toilet when travelling with children. Although not a parent myself, I could see the benefit of being able to seal the device after use and transport the contents to somewhere suitable before emptying and cleaning. I hadn't seen or heard of anything like that before.

If you were having a conversation with a mother either face to face or on the phone, how would you broach the subject?

"I am selling these great products would you like to take a look?" Here's where a piece of hypnotic programming comes along. The conscious mind has a barrier called critical thinking. In the previous statement your brain realises it is being sold to and immediately invokes your critical thinking. You automatically turn the positive of the question into a dubious thought. From that moment on, the name of the game is changing the prospects mind back to positive before having any chance of closing the sale. Trying to change a person's initial impression is a long and tedious road.

What would happen if you said as part of the conversation?

"The other day, I had one of those mornings where everything went wrong. My car broke down and I had to take two small children on the London Underground with an overnight bag, it was a nightmare."

I believe most mothers would empathise with your situation and want to know more. You continue.

"...and I had one of those moments where my youngest just needed to go to the toilet and you know what's its like…..[pause for dramatic effect]… no toilet when you need one."

If you have the attention of the person, the response can only be.

"What did you do?"

At this point the prospect is entirely engaged in the conversation. The first rule of hypnotic interaction is grab the attention of the person you want to work with and in this example the prospect is engulfed in curiosity, perfect.

"Well it wasn't a problem because I had this disposable toilet with me."

Developing curiosity as an emotional state is a powerful way to develop the need within the bounds of a normal conversation.

SCOTSMAN. By taking your deals though the SCOTSMAN method of evaluation you can identify a qualified prospect that is highly likely to close. For it to work properly be critical of the knowledge you have, if you cheat you are only cheating yourself. Look at the deal and ask yourself the questions from each letter. Give yourself a yes or a no. Don't settle for maybes or the in-betweens.   We are looking for deals that have a minimum of 4 yeses out of 7 plus the need. In most cases, without the need you really have no chance of taking an order.

If you don't manage to get a high score on the first call, aim to find out the things you don't know on the second call. For example, if you don't know who the decision maker is spend a little time before the next call and practise what to say to gain that information.

How do you know you've achieved if you haven't set a target
This key to success is true in just about anything you set out to do in sales or otherwise. If you get to work in the morning and state that you are going to do a session of telemarketing, how will you know if it was worthwhile?

You need to know why you are going to expend this effort, because if the real reason is, because your boss told you to do it then what satisfaction is in it for you. Ultimately, when you make a sale, the euphoria from the culmination of the sales process puts you on a high and you have something to show for your efforts by means of extra profit or commission. But there is a lot of calling and hard work to do before this happens. If you aimlessly go about the role of telemarketer without defined goals, the level of distractions within the business will be too great. You will be at the mercy of every person that wants to interrupt you. Without the end goal in your head it doesn't matter if you stop and talk or deal with other more important stuff and giving the telephone less than first priority will not amount to success.

The question is how big do you want to think?

According to Napoleon Hill's book we should all Think and Grow Rich! And this is true. The end goal should be clear to you. Is it a house with no mortgage, the ability to travel around the world exactly when the mood takes you because you have the funds or enough wealth to run your own business and employ people? Whatever you choose your actions have to start somewhere. As Tony Robbins states in Get the Edge on the subject of making it big, take massive action now.

To be practical for the moment, keep at the back of your mind the big things you want in life, cement those pictures in your subconscious and dream about them. The subconscious has no critical thought patterns and will begin to take you towards these goals as long as they are within the realms of possibility. What you have to do is understand what the first step is, nothing else. Planning is great, but too much planning is a procrastination in itself. Know what the first step towards your goal is and take massive action to do something now.

Sales ratio

As a telemarketer, you will either be issued a sales target or will need to set your own figures in line with your business plan. Most business plans will show a selection of projections over the course of a year, but let's take for example, the following data:

- At the end of the first year you want to have achieved £24,000 in new turnover

- You divide this amount by 12 to get £2,000 per month

- There are on average 21 days each month, giving you £95 a day to achieve

- An average sale for your company is £285

- You need 7 sales a month

These figures are rounded up and specifically basic so that you can follow the calculations. I would always use Microsoft Excel to hold the target so everything self calculates for ease. By breaking the overall sales target down into individual days we will know exactly what we have to do to achieve. There is no point having a monthly target and not knowing until the last day of the month what your actual figure is before you try to correct your underachievement, or you will always be playing catch up.

Assumptions

Notice that the sales ratio figures are all exact amounts. We know to the penny what we have to do. Our business plan has been designed to show what turnover and profit we have to do to stay in business and the sales manager has issued an appropriate target based on what sales have happened historically and the amount of business the company needs to do to employ the telemarketer and supporting staff.

I am going to tell you now, that a day target is still too large. As a professional telemarketer it is your responsibility to use your time effectively or face not earning commission and being under target. This role is like no other in a business. You determine what a priority task is and pursue a measured outcome. Wasted time is money you don't put in your pocket. If you are doing a telemarketing role and it isn't your first choice, reconsider now. This is a vital nerve of a growing business and your role in its success is assured as long as you fight tooth and nail for your time.

For a telemarketing professional to hit those figures and make it big, they need to make certain assumptions, which over a period of time transform into reliable data. These are:

- The number of calls you need to make to generate one sale
- The average length of the sales cycle
- The average length of the call

If you are new to a telemarketing role you will want to best guess the assumptions above. The first item is useful in motivation terms. All I have to do is make 100 calls and a sale will come in. The longer you are immersed in the world of a professional telemarketer the more you will be able to prove your assumptions and rely on this detail.

The average length of the sales cycle will differ depending on the product or service that you offer. Having sold software in the accounting industry I can attest to a sales cycle where the majority of business would close somewhere between 9 and 24 months. Whereas, with smaller, less technical items such as cosmetics as an example, a telemarketing person can expect to see revenue from the very first call. Until we have made a number of calls our assumptions are worthless.

The average length of call will be explained in greater detail later in this book. At the moment let's just say that if we were to call our contact database to establish a decision maker and their email address, this type of call would certainly take place rather more rapidly than a full fact finding mission.

The sales ratio and assumptions in practise
I am going to assume in my predictions below that you are using the telephone in the daytime between 9am and 5pm. I appreciate that this is not true for all telemarketers especially those that create opportunities in the realm of the general public as opposed to business to business communication. Use the same style of thinking and transpose the timings as appropriate.

Let's take the last thing on Friday (in fact every night) before you leave work. Be ready for the next day. Preparation will set you apart from your other telemarketing colleagues and office workers. You will need to decide:

- Which data are you calling?

- What type of calls are you making?

- How many calls of that type are you going to make?

The data you are calling is really important. Do you have at least or even more records than the target for the days calling? Always aim to exceed your estimates and targets, this will allow for those days when things might not go to plan for whatever reason. Make sure that your data has all of the basic information. Name, address, phone number and email address. I will discuss CRM, or customer relationship management software a little later in this book. A good supporting platform will allow you to hold information on all of the conversations you have instigated and any supporting documentation. For instance, if you are selling motorcycles you may find it advantageous to discuss and record the prospects preferences in terms of trade publication and style of motor bike. With this information in the database you are essentially turning a cold record into warm marketing.

The types of call can range from:

- A cleaning call, where you establish useful information like the name of the decision maker, email address and potential need for your product or service.

- Cold calls to fact find and generate contact with the decision maker.

- Warm calls, where an initial conversation has taken place or that a prospect has approached your business for additional information.

- Account management call, this is where you have already conducted business with this person and are looking for additional ways to up or cross sell.

So let's say, we have relatively poor data and the type of call is a cleaning call. The format of the call is short and we can assume that it is possible to make 100 calls in our eight hour working day. Our preparation is to print off a sheet which allows us to tally the number of times we dial in the day.

It sounds odd doesn't it? Tally? Tally isn't a modern word, is it? I am talking about putting a piece of paper beside the computer and making a tally mark after each call you make and this is why I want you to do that. When you look at the time and the number of tally's you have made, you will know hour on hour if you are going to make it. Let's take the one hundred cleaning calls in our example.

There is no point walking in at 9am and spending 10 minutes making a coffee, 5 minutes catching up on the football and 10 minutes checking emails before you start. You are killing yourself. Having just wasted the first hour of the day, you have condemned your first day of calling to underachievement and set yourself up to fail. Your target of one hundred calls is more likely to be seventy calls by the end of the day and although it's a reasonable effort, reasonable efforts don't exceed targets.

This is what you do. Get in early, at least ten minutes before everyone else. Make a drink and get to your desk, put your head set on and make the first call at 9am. If you are a home worker then procrastination is as big a threat as it is in the office. The distractions of walking the dog, breakfast TV and another slice of toast are all too real.

Think of your day in these terms.

- By 10am, 10 calls done.

- By 11am, 20 calls done. (push for 25)

- By midday, 30 calls (more like 40 or 50)

Get to the half way mark with extra fuel in the tank, always know that you can exceed.

At the end of the day, take these figures and enter them into your spreadsheet. This is an ideal place for a discerning telemarketer to begin to work magic and begin to turn assumptions into hard facts and averages. Then, before you go home, do what you do at the end of every evening, decide on your data, type of call and number of calls you are going to make.

The tally system
None of this works if you don't have a manual system of paperwork that you studiously record your effort on. I'm sure, there are whiz kids out there that can buy or write an application for their iPhones which will do this for you, but it isn't quite the same. By going through the procedure of manually writing on the sheet after each call you brain is constantly aware of where you are right now. The moment you hide the results away this motivation is lost.

Day	Calls	DM's	Apt's	Notes
	ⅢⅢ ⅢⅢ	ⅢⅢ IIII	II	(Emersons, call back 2pm)
	ⅢⅢ ⅢⅢ			Data from Chamber Mag
	ⅢⅢ ⅢⅢ			

I have always recorded three items as I make the call:

- The number of calls in the day. I use this as a motivation to over achieve my estimates and assumptions. I say count the no's, because our next sale will be clearly defined by our no of calls to sale ratio.

- DM's or decision makers. It's Okay making the calls, but to really accelerate success it is important to tally each time you speak to the person with real authority. This information acts as a safety and gives you an indication of the quality of your database information. If this figure is on the low side, then you may face a drought of closed business.

- Appointment or sale. Depending on your types of product, make a tally when you hit the end goal for you. In service related or professional service type organisations, the actual sales closing may be the responsibility of the new business sales person and not the telemarketer. In this case the end goal will always be getting an appointment. With retail or business products, the end goal may be the sale.

The benefits of time management

Few people in sales ever achieve complete perfection in time management for the simple reason that there are so many things that can disrupt your best intensions. Trying to be a salesman in a small business can be challenging as a new crisis can affect your priority and vastly reduce the number of calls and kill your motivation. By planning and recording your working patterns you can instantly take action to get back on target.

In the role of the telemarketer you have the best possible chance to lay your stall out and define success. Whether you work alone, are in a small business or part of a large call centre, put your figures on the wall beside you. State the case in no uncertain terms. This is what I aim to do, this is what I am doing and this will be the result if I do. Any deviation from this regime, such as meetings, trainings, role swaps etc will all impact on the final result, the company simply cannot afford it.

Now I know more than anyone that training is vital. The more product knowledge you have and telemarketing skill you can muster, the more success you will generate. Be sensible. Book the training over a working lunch, or last thing in the evening or listen to an audio recording in the car on the way to work. If you know you have an hour at the end of the day when you cannot make calls, then push to achieve your target before this begins. An extra 5% a day will make allowances for days which simply don't go to plan.

As a telemarketer your role includes convincing your managers and superiors that you know exactly what you are doing. Get in the habit of reviewing your figures as often as once a week. Show that you are a valued member of the company, that your contribution is tangible and measured. Create a spreadsheet and show them:

- The number of calls you make in a day and the monthly totals

- How many decision makers you spoke to

- How many appointments you made

- How many sales you made and the total value, include profit figures if you have them

- Use the power of the spreadsheet to generate proof, how many calls to an order, how many decision makers to an order

This proof is your meal ticket to more money, either as a senior person in the team, a manager, an account manager and new business representative are all possibilities if you show this aptitude. Hypnotists are always taught to see a situation from three possible angles before making any decisions to make change. This is a particularly useful technique in any social interaction. Look at a situation from your standpoint, what information are you collecting using your eyes, ears and importantly your feelings or intuition. Then imagine the same situation through the eyes of the person you are speaking to. Are they calm, on board, in rapport with you, would you say you are both congruently seeing eye-to-eye on a topic and finally, the third position. Imagine stepping back and watching the interaction from a complete stranger's point of view. A presupposition in NLP – Neuro Linguistic Programming is that there are no bad clients, only poor communicators. Be more critical of what you say and do and get in the habit of listening to your conversations.

I say this for the simple reason, that if you work for someone or have a manager, imagine how they look at you and the role of the telemarketer because most companies at one point in their past will have dabbled with telemarketing and decided that the return on investment for them was less than expected. Few of them will have keep performance records in the way that we have spoken about leaving the employed telemarketer out on a limb, living in an environment in which they have no say in possible outcomes. If you keep good records you can account for your contribution to the business. If you have made sales, shout about them. Put your totals up and shout about success.

We all want more money. We may even get a small annual increase in line with inflation, but this is not going to float the boat of a person with dreams and defined goals. You want to be in a position that your work is so valuable, you gain the respect of the people directly above you, the manager and the owner. This will come over time. Keep recording the numbers and success is just around the corner.

In one company I worked, the management team decided to set up a new division. We all worked in one office only a few feet apart. The existing team had seen successful when times were good, but as the recession had taken hold, targets were often underachieved. In the new team, myself and the manager, a guy who in actual fact did step up and actually did some calling himself, created a target and sales ratio. We placed a large white board directly in front of the main office door which no one could ignore. We plotted our progress and statistics and before long the management team were discussing how the two teams could be generating such differing figures.

On one occasion, I had posted a number of 125 calls in a single day, a figure that far exceeded anything that been achieved before. After investigation it turned out that the other team considered sending individual emails out to prospects a useful part of their time, where our team relied on the use of the phone to get the results. The moral of this story is that the management made decisions based on emotion and the sales figures of the day that is all. When the new team was set up the sales ratio and activity numbers proved our concept. Imagine this, the management team approaching you and asking for advice on the best way forward, be studious these figures will give you that.

The pipeline
The sales pipeline is how we forecast, how we work out in a small business what money is going to come in this month and in a larger business what business we have to cover our costs and exceed targets.

We spoke earlier about the saying telemarketing is a numbers game and in many ways it is. In many of the company's in which I've worked the preferred method of pipeline reporting was the sales funnel. Imagine a large clear plastic funnel with a wide throat and narrow pipe at the bottom. As you sell things in your business they appear at the narrow pipe at the bottom. In reality, you have had to quote a lot of activity to make this sale. The earlier stages of the sale form the wider part of the funnel.

- At the top of the funnel, the cold section, an area of literally thousands of companies that you have yet to call. Sometimes known as suspects, if qualified for size in SCOTSMAN.

- Below that, with fewer prospects, the warm section, people that you have spoken to and have yet to show definitive interest in your product or service.

- Below that, with even fewer numbers and getting narrower all the time, the hot section, a list of qualified prospects that meet your SCOTSMAN criteria and have indicated a timescale to purchase.

- Then in the narrowest part of the funnel, the sold section where we have the newly named customers.

In a modern CRM – customer relationship management system, the labels of cold, warm, hot, sold and lost are appended to each record during each part of the sale. Quite often, a business will increase the number of stages adding complexity to this system. These additions aren't always responsible for adding clarity to the situation. For instance, cold, meeting attended, proposal written, sold and lost. The labels can say and mean anything, please make sure that all the telemarketers you employ interpret the labels in the same way.

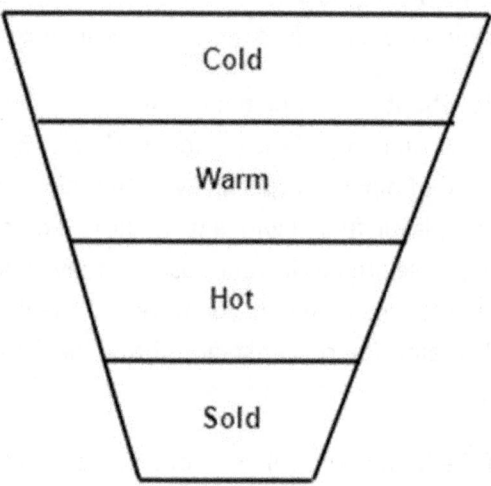

All well and good I hear you say. The records in our pipeline are classified and we can keep track of them in terms of stages of the sale. One of the problems with a sales funnel pipeline is that you are dealing with an ever increasing number of data records at any one time. The more you do, the more you convert is a type of approach that is not always the most sensible. To be highly successful we need to learn to focus on the prospects which have the best opportunity to close, by working smarter, not harder.

In the following example, the sales pipeline, you don't actually enter a prospect into the pipe until it has been qualified using your SCOTSMAN criteria, 4 out of 7 plus the need. In this case, you are presenting your manager a forecast containing a lot less information, but because you have qualified the possible order, taking into account whether they have the budget, a compelling need and authority to purchase, you stand a better chance of stating when the order is going to arrive.

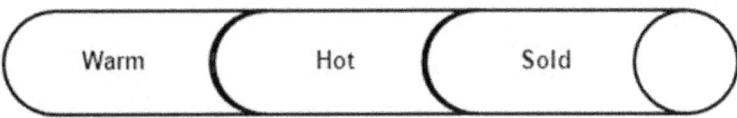

In life, some orders you have been promised are delayed for all manner of perfectly acceptable reasons and these in your pipeline will show a deficit in your forecasting. Which isn't great lets face it, if you tell your boss you are going to bring in £10,000 worth of orders and you only bring in £5,000, it doesn't look good for you or your abilities to forecast. What you don't want to start doing though is enter prospects into your pipeline that haven't been rigorously qualified using SCOTSMAN or you stand the chance of creating a real nightmare. More telemarketers are fired off the back of poor forecasting than for any other reason. Think about this scenario again. You forecast £20,000 and only a fraction of that comes in, it looks like you don't know what is going on. The reason is the prospect's promises will not transpire the way you want them to unless you have asked the right questions and tied them down. You have left the opportunity so wide open that it may or may not come in. At the other end of the scale if you predict £5,000 and £20,000 comes in, although nice, it does little to raise your kudos.

Get in the habit of updating the prospects SCOTSMAN with every conversation. Make a point of filling in the blanks, if you have any, every time you call. You may call them for something small to confirm a colour or particular pattern and have a prepared question ready to complete your investigation, say some thing like:

"Oh, while I'm still on the phone, I forgot to ask you, will any of your colleagues be consulted on this item, do I need to let them have samples?"

The telemarketer is probing for additional information on the authority of the prospect.

It is good practise to take a snapshot of your pipeline each month and compare it with the record of last month. Try to identify which orders are sticking and re-evaluate your SCOTSMAN. This is a great technique for the sales manager. You will soon get lost in the myriad of promises in an extensive pipeline document, make a note of them and question why the deal hasn't completed. Quite simply, ask your telemarketers the SCOTSMAN questions. I always have a separate section called the 'Happy Place' to allow for those prospective orders that defy all attempts to tie them down. This is a place of gut feel. If I really think it will happen at some point it stays there under scrutiny. As a general rule of thumb:

- Cold – this is a holding location for records that have yet to be cleaned, indefinite timescale.

- Warm – records may also stay here indefinitely, as long as a scheduled call is present.

- Hot – the stage before the order comes in. No prospect should remain here for more than a month.

- Sold – the reference only refers to the first sale of a business. Remember when they become your customer, the process starts again and you can return them to warm for additional marketing and cross sell purposes.

- Lost – When you lose a sale, don't linger on what could have been, you won't win them all. Analyse the outcome using SCOTSMAN and learn from anything you could have done better. Accept the outcome and put the record back into warm for recycling

The importance of great data

Give yourself a head start and use the best possible data you can find. It is so difficult to precisely know how to grade the data you are calling until you had a chance to test and record the calling statistics and ratios. It seems to be the passion of a business owner to hold onto their suspect and prospect data for as long possible. Be sure that when you begin to work you mark each record in someway to keep track of what has been called and the reasons why you chose it.

Say for example, you are a company based in London and over the years you have amassed a large of amount of data from all manner of sources. This happens. A sales person may join the business and bring their customer list, mailing lists may be purchased, barcodes have been scanned at an exhibition and all of that information goes to make up your prospect data.

Start with the size part of your SCOTSMAN profile for your business and understand the type of companies and sectors you want to attract. You may choose all of the postcodes within the M25 (the London orbital ring road), an industry type, perhaps the industry type of printing and copying with a turnover of between £1 million and £5 million. Again, these figures are given as an example. Adjust them appropriately for your target marketplace.

In addition to recording your sales ratios and activity data, make a note each time you find a record where the company no longer exists or the decision making contact is no longer in situ. It can be assumed that over a period of time some companies will have closed, moved or merged with other businesses. The telephone numbers will either not work or a new company name will be entered off the back of what you find out from the contact. If you record each occasion of this within your call statistics you can build averages to support theories of how poor the data really is.

In terms of the decision maker, you can also assume that an occurrence of them leaving or changing roles within a business will not be reflected in older data. I say assume. This is an assumption it is not a fact. If you do not keep accurate records from each day's calling you are on a sticky wicket. A poor quality telemarketer will always complain about the quality of the data, in the same way a sales man will always complain about the quality of leads that have been given to him. Without statistics taken over a period of time your protestations will be thankless.

So where can you source data. Sourcing data costs money. Unless of course, a generous donor has gifted your business a limitless list of prospects, all of it costs you in one way or the other. Let's take the simplest way. To find a directory either online or printed of the types of companies you want to sell to. This can either be a trade publication, an exhibition listing or a website filtered for the purpose. In all of these examples the time to enter the data in your database should not be underestimated. It takes a long time to put a record together with the name of the company, the address, industry type, telephone number, turnover and contact names at the very least. Entering data does not make you money, it sinks time and if you take this route it will account for at least half of your working time. There may be a couple of occasions a year where this is your only way to input data such as a trade association listing or a collection of business cards from an exhibition and these are contacts that you do not want to miss. If you enter data manually it is unusual for the correct contact and their email address to be present, an additional cost is incurred calling the company to clean the record. Email addresses are efficient marketing collateral.

Make referrals count. If you sign a customer and he is happy with your work ask for the names of other companies like his, then add them to your database and call them. This is highly effective warm marketing.

You can also buy the names and addresses of specific companies and sectors. There are hundreds of suppliers on the internet all claiming to have a unique way of collecting data and they all make claims as to its quality. This is complex and costly, although if you get it right you have a higher percentage chance of getting to your target market quicker, hence creating more opportunities. Things you should look out for:

Opt in emailing capability

If you are considering purchasing data, aim to get the maximum possible use out of it. Collaborative marketing means that you capitalise on contact using a selection of means, not only the telephone. Email marketing is really effective and is a measured approach, so ask for the email address when you define the criteria. If you use a web service for this, the online company will supply click and open reports so that you can see exactly which prospects took an interest in what you sent. A call to these records means you are calling a warm market, not cold data. When speaking to the supplier you will hear the phrase opt-in emails or double opt-in. This means that the prospect has said they are happy to receive emails from them or their sub contractors. If you don't get permission and you send a message to unknown accounts, this is known as spam email and you are at risk of fines and being blacklisted by your ISP – internet service provider. A correctly policed opt-in policy by the supplier means that the prospect only receives a small amount of wanted mail each month.

TPS – telephone preference service

In the United Kingdom, the law states that companies that do not want to receive unsolicited calls may register on the telephone preference service. An unsolicited caller is then at risk of a fine for breaching these rules. Again, there are many on line TPS services so that you can check each number you call for legitimacy. When you buy data you can ask that only the records that are not on the TPS be extracted. This will save you time. Remember though, a client may choose to sign up at any time. Make sure that the numbers you are calling are rechecked every thirty days.

Expiry on use

You will find restrictions on data, especially where email addresses are concerned. The most commons ones are, no record to emailed more than once a month and no more than nine times in a year. It can even expire to the extent that after the year, any record you have been unable to contact should be removed from your database and not used, however if a prospect has requested information these may be pursued in the usual way.

Seeded records

Purchased records will often contain a series of false records which are used to track the restriction of the database. You can sometimes find these in the process of your calling, but not always.

In small business or where the data you are using is suspected poor quality, use a cleaning call and research to save time. In this I am saying use the internet and enter the name of the company, read blogs and the information held on free credit checking web sites. Make an initial call and speak to the receptionist or first contact and ask some basic questions to satisfy the Size in SCOTSMAN. Try these:

"I am looking to send your finance director an invite to our yearly road show in June, can I just confirm a number of points before I do?"

[wait for the yes or okay]

"I'd like ask, the numbers of employees on this site?"

[wait for the answer]

"...and the current software package you use for accounts?"

[wait for the answer].

"Thank you for that, it helps our marketing team forward the correct information and who should I send this to?"

[check the email address]

If you get any resistance whatsoever, be honest and polite, thank them for the time and put the phone down.

It is good practise to ring as many company's as you can, but don't make six calls to a single business before you find out they are too small. The decision maker will often be the most guarded person, so use any contact you can to give you background as early as possible.

CRM – Customer Relationship Management

Using software adds an enormous amount of control to your prospect interactions.   There are many types of CRM package and without offering a study on each individually I am going to list some of the more useful features you might like to consider.

- A database that contains the main company, name address and contact details. In most cases, additional fields can be added to store specific data. You may want to sort your prospects by car drivers and bus users, or by the age of the client or preference of pizza topping. You simply add the new database field, populate a list with the various options you may encounter and when you have the discussion with the person, mark off the answer in the CRM. When the data is stored you simply sort or filter all of your prospects using your predefined selections.

- A dated and timed record of every conversation you have. Especially when your sales cycle is anything from 9 months to 2 years you will want to make a note of everything that has been said.

- The ability to enter a call back, a reminder that pops up on screen or in a list to remind you to contact the prospect. This is the work horse engine of the telemarketer, on average 50% of the data that you will call in a day comes from this feature.

- All marketing emails, standard emails, letters and documents that you have sent or received are stored in the CRM for you to view at anytime. Some packages will automatically synchronise your existing email system with the CRM.

- Mail shots and electronic marketing are sent from within the CRM and each prospect record will display the impact and success of that mailing with your contact. Mail shots created in Microsoft Word when printed are attached to the prospect record for full traceability.

- To save time the TAPI – telephone application programmer interface will allow you to dial your telephone from the computer screen. When you are making 100 calls a day this is a time saver.

- The records can be viewed on your mobile phone. There are times when you are out of the office for whatever reason. Having the same functionality on a smart phone can help you stop missing important deadlines.

- Multi-user functionality. Centralising your efforts on a server is what all larger call teams should aspire to. CRM will offer useful printed reports and dashboards of information as standard and these become even more educational when they contain comparisons between telemarketing colleagues.

- Remember that the CRM system is not just for the telemarketing team. It is a valuable resource for employees to record every conversation and service call.

Creating a compelling unique business presentation

The importance of product knowledge

If you hook the interest and curiosity of a prospect using a structured approach, you will inevitably have in it in your plan to explain the many benefits of owning or using your product or service. In fact, I would suggest that you will want to leave spaces for the prospect to ask questions that you can easily answer. As they think of these questions and deliver them, you will be able to identify if the prospect is serious about your offering, whereas if prolonged periods of silence prevail it is almost impossible to receive any practical feedback. Of course, in a face to face meeting it is easy to see that the prospect is uneasy with certain aspects of your presentation or that they are listening avidly. Using the telephone we do need to improve our levels of hearing along with questioning techniques. This is yet another area where your sensory perception is required to evaluate if the prospect is ready to move to the next stage. There is simply no reason to offer them pricing if they have no need for the product or if expenditure is out of the question. Still using SCOTSMAN as guidance, punctuate your conversation with predefined questions. You will often hear a professional telemarketer use this type of strategy.

"Our drink is made from over eighty five percent pure Aloe Vera and only natural components. The Aloe plant has been used for thousands of years for its medicinal and healing properties and is best known with its label, the burns plant. Can I ask you Samantha, are foreign holidays something that you like to take?"

In this rather simple example the telemarketer has given a piece of information about a product. We all do it, we inform people about our product and exciting properties because that's what we are passionate about. What most of us fail to do is shut up, take a breath and ask for feedback. In this text, it shows that we have given a little piece of information, the prospect has listened carefully (and we can only imagine what they are thinking at that point) and we have stopped and asked a question. It is really important that you ask a question and then shut up and listen. The feedback you get is the purpose of the communication, do you remember that?

The prospect is either going to say yes, I love holidays and I often get burnt or no I don't like hot climates. What they say is not really important, it is the way it is said that you are listening for. Do they sound enthusiastic, are they asking the sorts of questions that interested people ask or do they simply want to know the price and get off the line.

I go on to say this, know your product, its specification, where it can be used, how it works, what colours and sizes it comes in, what celebrities have tried it, anything that will make you an expert. As a telemarketer you want to become someone's trusted advisor, the person they come to for honest, sound advice. Don't make false claims about a product, stay away from unsubstantiated reasoning, be honest to yourself and be honest with the prospect.

The important fact is information is power, use it sparingly. Have a route through your product presentation that has a selection of questions woven into the framework that allow the prospect to speak. Get their opinion. Appreciate their point of view, because the customer is always right. That's right, even when they are completely wrong and ill informed, the fault is not with the customer it is with the telemarketer that has yet to communicate and influence the prospect into seeing their point of view. This concept is objection handling and will be detailed in the next chapter.

When you are taking the call and the prospect asks a question that you either cannot answer or in your opinion could have been answered in a better way, write it down. Add these questions to your arsenal of preparation. In reality, if we make enough calls we can prepare for almost every eventuality. Take this example, if you get invited to an interview for your dream job, what is the best way to prepare for success?

- Write down all the questions you think they will ask you.

- Work out the answers to all of the questions above.

- Work out all the questions you are going to ask. This means that in 80% of cases you are prepared for almost every eventuality and will need to use your own flair and personality for the last 20%. Telemarketing is no different. In the next chapter, we will look at this kind of preparation in detail.

Take product training sessions seriously. When a supplier takes you through the product, listen carefully and take notes and always ask the contact:

- What are the three main selling features of the product?

- What are the benefits of these features in a normal working environment?

- What sorts of questions do your customers ask you?

The value proposition
We've spoken in the previous chapter that a prospect will buy your product or service for two reasons, they have a specific need or that a desire exists to own the item. In the former example, a specific need, your approach needs to encapsulate the following procedure:

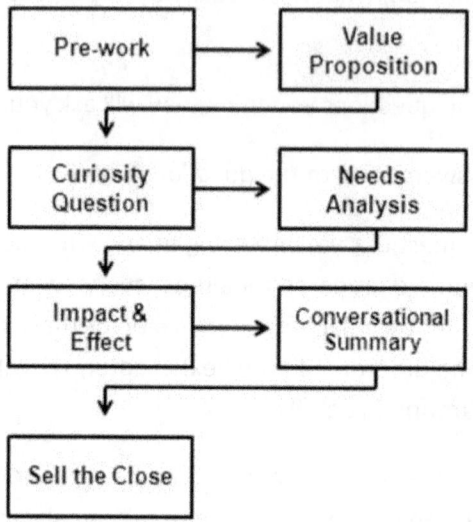

Pre-work. It goes without saying that it is difficult to grab the attention of the prospect in the first place, so you need a strategy to hold their attention and meet their requirements not yours. Let's look at a successful structure that typifies the correct way to approach a new prospect. We'll start with pre-work. We touched on the importance of good data a few pages ago. If you have a selection of records to choose from then it is prudent to pre-qualify them before launching an onslaught. Like I said before, why ring a prospect six times and then realise they are not appropriate for your style of business. I am referring to the Size in SCOTSMAN, our defined market. Of course, if you have purchased data and eliminated all records that fall outside of this assessment, the majority of work is already done.

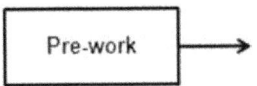

For our pre-work we are going to notate an overview of the business. The more we know about the business, the more opportunities we have to open lines of interesting dialogue. There are six elements to a business. These are finances, vision, business model, route to market, structure and trading partners. By breaking down our information into these six areas we can be critical of our overview and decide if we know sufficient information before making the call.

Draw three lines onto an A4 sheet in the following way and name each box as shown:

Finance	Vision
Model	Route to Market
Structure	Trading Partners

The finances panel is where we understand where the business is now and its recent history, so you can imagine turnover for the last 5 years would be enormously valuable. As a telemarketer you run the risk of alienating the prospect during the call if you use too many probing questions in the area of finance alone.

"What is your turnover now?" is a question with sharp edges that may do more to engage a person's critical thinking than relax them into offering more information.

The vision panel is asking the business where they are going in the next 5, 10 and 15 years. This is the juxtaposition to finances. Where are you now? (Finances) - Where are you going? (Vision) A brilliant question for a business owner is:

"Where do you see the business in the next 5 years?"

Any question that you ask in the future tense adds to your professionalism. Try:

"How do you see this market changing?"

or "In your opinion, what do you think is the best approach for someone new to the industry?"

Successful businesses have passionate leaders that have opinions they love to share. This is why sales people get into sales, for the opportunity to talk and be inspired by others. Make conversation, take an interest, but what ever you do don't begin selling anything.

Questions about the vision of the business evoke emotion and people don't change their minds or are influenced unless emotion is involved. The game of sales is about changing and moving the state of the individual to get them to appreciate your point of view. Creating a high state of emotion is where big decisions are made in a heartbeat because they feel right. I will agree that they have to be supported by quantities of real proof and return on investment calculations and the like, but procrastination is eradicated by emotion. A memorable statement is, the last state before complete understanding is confusion, isn't that right? While we are taking in information and trying to make sense of it all, we may be enthused by the project and unable to make a decision until it all falls into place.

As you'll see in a moment, the first question we ask will rely on the questions ability to create an emotional state of curiosity, the most productive state of all. Great speakers do this all the time.

"Ladies and gentlemen, in a moment I'm going to let you into a little secret that made me an instant millionaire, but first let tell you about…"

The outcome of this approach is an interesting one. Either they will fall whole heartedly into the trap and listen intently or fade away uninterested, here lies the first principal of the telemarketer, know when to proceed and know when to stop.

The next panel, business model asks the question:

"What do you do?"

The answer simply tells us, the exact things that a business does to make profit. Remember, keep questioning, a business may have more than one income stream. An owner may tell you that they do pizzas and flat breads, you may clarify the situation and learn that pizzas account for 90% of the revenue. By having an understanding of the products or services, it will make it easier for your match your proposition to their specific need.

Route to market. How do they sell? The prospect may not deal directly with the end user and may choose a reseller or distribution approach. Web sites may be their main form of income or sales may accumulate through a retail outlet. All of these methods create challenges in life and challenges need solutions – does anyone out there have a solution for sale?

The structure panel is asking for information about location. Do they attract international, national or local business? How many locations do they operate from? How many people work on site or remotely? Now you may be thinking the things I sell won't benefit from knowing this, but don't be so sure. I appreciate if you sell mobile phones, this information is pretty vital to understanding your potential in the sale.

However, if all you sell is sandwiches and want to do business in the local area, continue to ask the questions. The information may still prove valuable in conversational terms which we'll cover in greater detail shortly.

Finally, the trading partners panel. Find out, who they do business with, famous names, large customers, speciality suppliers. Prospects are always influenced by associates, governing bodies, accountants and auditors, Chamber of Commerce, Chamber of Trade, consultants, all of which influence their buying decision. If you have accurate information in each of the six panels you are well on the way to understanding your prospect.

The prospects web site is always a good place to start to get an overall impression of the business, although a poorly written or expensive web site may not accurately portray the true trading situation. It is an ideal place to understand what they do and the types of customers they trade with. Look out for the names of directors and managers in the case studies and any news items showing that the business is expanding.

With larger companies you may also want to search the internet on the many web sites that offer financial and statistical information, again many of these offer limited amounts of information for free. The turnover, profitability, number of employees, the names of the directors can all be found on the right web sites.

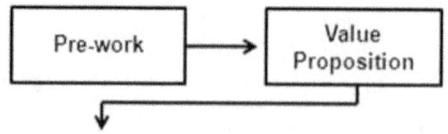

Value Proposition. Now let's look at what you do as a business? It's difficult for me to imagine all of the products and services you could all be selling, there are thousands of combinations. I'm going to use a couple of companies I know as examples. First of all:

1. Write down what it is you sell

2. Identify what it is that marks out your business as special

The following company sells IT hardware, I'm sure the list of products and services will be familiar to all of us.

- Computers and printers – hardware
- Outsourced helpdesk support
- On site engineers
- Repair workshop

I have specifically kept this example simple. When you do this exercise for yourself, go to town and write down everything you do.

Now stage 2. What is it that marks out you business as special. A computer company is more difficult than most when it comes to answering this question. I'm sure there are lots of them in the area and differentiation is hard to clarify. Dig deep and write down even the obscure answers you are coming up with.

- I have two engineers who have worked for me for thirty years
- Our workshop turns around repairs in 24 hours
- We support our clients at weekends and over Christmas
- Our support contracts include the cost of parts and labour

These unique selling points are only unique in certain circumstances depending on the context. If you say to a prospect we are unique we work on Sundays, he may think we are closed at the weekend so I don't care. However, a small supermarket or retail shop may find this hook useful in deed. At this moment, all we are trying to do is find as many interesting things to talk about when we make the call.

Here's another example. A bicycle shop, situated on the banks of a public access reservoir.

Stage 1. What do they do?

- Sell bicycles from three main manufacturers
- Repair centre for bikes
- Hire centre for bikes
- Accessories, coats, hats, shoes, etc

Stage 2. What is unique and special about what you do?

- The only reseller of X-racers in the county
- The only hire bikes at the reservoir, no public roads
- Free accessories that can be claimed on new purchases and hire

You should now take a sheet of A4 paper and draw a line down the middle. Mark the left hand section with what do you do? And the right hand section, my USP's (unique selling points). It seems an easy exercise after all this is your business. Certainly the left hand panel will roll off the tongue quickly, think carefully and write everything down. The right hand section will be a little harder. I am asking you to differentiate and tell me what is unique about you in some way. Remember the ability to think about a situation from three different angles, through your eyes, through the eyes of your prospect and from a person on the outside looking in. When you write down a personal, company or product quality that is unique, scrutinise it from all three angles. When you discuss this point, will its uniqueness satisfy the contact or create scepticism or misunderstanding?

The mistake most telemarketers make is that they lead with these unique things. Take this example.

"Mr Cooper we have an award winning ham and orange pie and I'd like to make an appointment to come and speak to you about it."

So, your objective is to make an appointment and sell pies, what is the prospects goal? Come on. Look at the situation through their eyes. They have agreed to take the call and you have one opportunity to get them curious about your unique idea, product or service. Does this question grab their attention in any way? Of course, not, when you listen to this question through the ears of the prospect you can hear:

- A salesman trying to sell something (I can hear you say 'but Steve, I am a sales person. You're right you are, but don't start selling too soon)

- You have assumed that the contact is interested in pies and that they are the right contact

- You've presumed that they like to speak face to face to conduct business

Ever heard the saying ASSUME, it makes an ASS of U and ME. If you assume something, then you have a high possibility of getting it wrong. I'm sure most of you aren't mind readers in the circus, so why leave this simple skill of rapport to chance. By asking questions, you aren't assuming anything. The answers are giving you the detail you need.

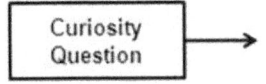

Curiosity Question. To kick proceedings off with the prospect we will of course, be polite and courteous on the phone, this goes without saying. What we then need is a way of asking a question that either hooks their interest leaving them wanting more or indicates to you that they cannot or are not willing to proceed.

Say our unique selling point is that your broadband or leased line packages are the fastest internet connection speed in the area. What question would excite the interest of the listener?

1. "Does your internet connection satisfy the needs of your people?"

2. "Can I ask, does your business have a plan for reducing its telephone charges?"

3. "I see that your business is located on two sites, do you mind me asking, do people in those locations spend a lot of time speaking on the telephone?"

4. "I wonder if you can help me, I'm dealing with a number of companies that use the internet for generating sales leads, is this something that comes under your remit?"

5. "I'm not sure if you can help me, but we've been installing high speed broadband on the site next to your company this week and I wondered if this might be of interest to you?"

6. "You might be able to help me. I'm looking for companies in this area that would like to move to faster broadband as it becomes available, is this something you'll be looking at?"

The opening prime desire or curiosity question is one of the few questions that you will actually script. It should be written and rehearsed out loud, well before you try it on the phone. Let's look at the writing first. If you are new to telemarketing or if English literature is not one of your favourite subjects, you may take more time writing the question than is truly needed. Be a little more pragmatic with your approach. The trick is to start writing immediately. The six examples above were brainstormed in around three minutes or so, no longer.

These phrases are not perfect by any means so we'll be looking at how we critique our work in a moment. The way you deliver these words is more important and actually defines their effectiveness. Some phrases you write will not sound natural to you when you speak them out loud, whereas other colleagues may find they are more palatable and work for them. Take this tip on board, write as many as you can. Have an arsenal of options to work from.

From the examples above, let's look at the techniques which you can use to critique your work. One of my favourite techniques is to soften the language. Earlier I explained that the conscious part of our brains contains our critical thinking, a filter that examines incoming information in the form of sound, pictures and smells and raises a barrier allowing you to feel sceptical or unconvinced. When you soften language you are essentially taking the critical thinking off line. You'll realise this when you meet someone for the first time in a social context. At first the conversation is quite stilted, until you gain rapport and feel comfortable with each other before opening up to deeper topics of conversation.

The phrase "I'm not sure if you can help me", is a great way to disengage critical thinking. Most people at the end of the phone are convinced you are trying to sell them something, but this phrase has the opposite effect. Most people are generous in spirit and are only too happy to help if you give them the chance.

"I wonder if you can help me?"

This is another good phrase and notice how on the page in words I've added a question mark. The way you deliver this phrase is vitally important. With a question mark, it becomes an immediate question to which you need an answer. There is no supporting information for the listener and they begin to second guess your intentions.

I wonder is you can help me?.............about what?

A great technique with language is to record both sides of the conversation and listen. If you listened to this example you would hear the question, a pregnant pause – in fact a gaping hole where the listeners conscious mind has the opportunity to think the worst and a bewildered response, about what?

Say the phrase again, this time as a statement. I wonder if you can help me. Only this time you say the phrase almost nonchalantly without emphasis and tag on the real reason for the call.

"I wonder if you can help me [a tiny breath], I'm dealing with a number of companies…."

This is exactly the reason why you say these patterns out loud. Not only is the English language the most technically complex of all communications, but the way the information is delivered is an art form in itself.

Notice, at the end of each of the examples I've written is a question mark. The purpose of the communication is the response that you get. This means that if you keep talking you miss knowing whether the prospect is interested or totally nonplussed. The same can be said if you write a sentence that is too long. The general rule of thumb is that you should be able to deliver the sentence in a controlled manner without losing breath. If it's too long change it, rewrite it and mix up your own examples to get one sentence you are going to try.

We have six examples written in the brainstorm, let's critique them individually.

1. "Does your internet connection satisfy the needs of your people?"

When I read this out loud and hear it, the effect it has on me is a stark and direct pattern of words. It stops me in my tracks. It makes me question the question and ultimately the need for the call. The end part of the sentence, 'the needs of your people' is also closed and could easily prompt the listener to say no, at which point you are stumped. In this case, I would look for a better question from my list, but this is not to say that this is a bad approach. If you have the character and the confidence, this approach may have a positive effect. We certainly cannot generalise and say all listeners will have these traits and at this stage of the call you are unlikely to have built sufficient rapport to read the prospect accurately.

2. "Can I ask, does your business have a plan for reducing its telephone charges?"

Remember the unique selling point of the host business is the fastest broadband internet in the area. So this question appears to side step the unique topic instead of hitting it head on. (For those that don't sell broadband, high speed versions can now be used to carry telephone calls and subsequent charges) The art of conversation does not stay in one place. It meanders under the manipulation of the telemarketer who probes all areas of detail looking for opportunity. As I said, the curiosity question is one of the only questions you script, the following questions flow freely depending on the conversation. You can imagine the call going something like this.

Telemarketer: "Can I ask, does you business have a plan for reducing its telephone charges?"

Prospect: "We always want to save money."

[Permission from the prospect to proceed]

Telemarketer: "What type of phone system do you use at the moment?"

Prospect: "An old one, we've had it for years."

[Don't assume, but new technology this isn't]

Telemarketer: "Have you researched any other types?"

Prospect: "Not really it's all a bit technical for us."

[He has just told you to keep it simple]

Telemarketer: "A lot of companies in your position would consider the internet..."

It all starts to roll from the initial curiosity question. You move with the client listening carefully to the answer. At this stage there is no selling going on you are just asking questions. The need is more important than the solution at this moment.

3. "I see that your business is located on two sites, do you mind me asking, do people in those locations spend a lot of time speaking on the telephone?"

Again, this is an indirect question and as a professional telemarketer you are attempting to discover the vision of the business. By finding a need and knowing the vision you are allowing your sales potential to soar. If you identify a problem for them say for instance, their gas bills are too high and you sell cheap gas you are on the way to making a sale. Imagine this, if you have already got them to tell you that their vision for growth includes taking over two other companies this year, then your opportunity has just trebled.

4. "I wonder if you can help me, I'm dealing with a number of companies that use the internet for generating leads, is this something that comes under your remit?"

I would hope in the pre-work phase of calling you would have identified the right decision maker, but nothing stops you from affirming this in person. It also allows the question to slip under the radar of critical thinking. Say the words out loud. The conscious part of your mind can only process a number of items at one go, somewhere between 5 and 9. When we deliver a list vocally to a prospect and it is the first time they've heard it, it is difficult for them to remember each previous item. In fact in marketing the magic number is three, 123, ABC, etc. Try this, speak to a friend and list three things in the conversation. The mind remembers the third and begins to struggle on the second and has all but lost the first. Delivered correctly, tag questions are answered without thought. The tag being the final part of the phrase:

"Is this something that comes under your remit?"

5. "I'm not sure if you can help me, but we've been installing high speed broadband on the site next to your company this week and I wondered if this might be of interest to you?"

I've said before most people are happy to help, so by saying I'm not sure if you can help me, stops them from thinking about you as a sales person and more as someone that needs advice. In this example, we are also invoking the referral principle. Aren't you just a bit nosey and like to know what your neighbours are buying. Maybe it's a business competitive advantage thing, they are a similar business to yours and you don't want to be left behind. Like I said before, a referral is warm business. A great way to end a negotiation is to say, I will accept these terms if you agree to speak to my next customer or offer me a quote I can use in a brochure.

6. "You might be able to help me, I'm looking for companies in this area that would like to move to faster broadband as it becomes available, is this something you'll be looking at?"

If I was the prospect it would sound to me like you are conducting a survey, not selling. Ask more questions, what speed does he need? Is the vision to grow the business, what speed will they want then?

Feel free to use any of the examples above and play with them, but don't get stuck on them. You have developed your own structure of the English language and the words will be different in different market places. You wouldn't speak the same if you were selling surf boards or insurance, would you?

Write your ideas down. This is the value proposition, this is meant to be worked on, rewritten and written again, we are not at the free style section yet. Record yourself saying the words and listen to it. Put yourself in the position of the prospect and understand how they would respond. Learning to analyse and be critical of your own work is where the learning begins.

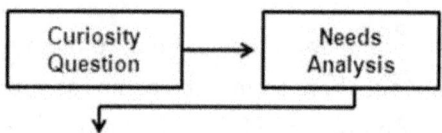

Needs Analysis. So far, our approach has been to prepare diligently, listen to the words we use, analyse them and rewrite for the greatest effect. With your curiosity question in place you will have motivated the prospect to either open up and begin speaking or follow the opposite route of going quiet on you. Whatever your question has been remain silent and don't jump into the space with another question. I know you will find the silence uncomfortable and as a telemarketer you are taught to speak at every opportunity, but now is the time to listen intently.

First of all, you are gauging the speed in which the prospect reacts. As a general rule of thumb, people speak at the same speed they process information. It doesn't make them any less intelligent, but it does mean that if you don't match this pattern it reduces the amount of rapport.

In the UK, we have a radio show called Desert Island Disks where famous people discuss their lives and introduce their favourite music. On one particular occasion the actor John Malkovich was interviewed. I remember the flavour of the questions expanding on the history of films he'd made, why he felt they were successful and how his contribution had helped. Now I get the feeling Malkovich is a deep thinker, a person of high intellect, who over the years of his career had learned to deeply analyse the roles he was asked to play, hence the high standard and quality of his work. The questions required him to go inside himself to analyse the whys, to produce the words which would be delivered to the programmes interviewer and this took time.

Now I can also see the interviewer's point of view. This is radio, the words count. Any spaces of silent interval aren't easily accounted for by the listener at home. The result was only partial answers. I'd like to think that the actor would spend five minutes on each answer, a performance of sorts giving the listener a highly detailed and accurate version of events.

This is how it sounded to me. The question was delivered, the first part of the answer spoken, a short pause while he processed the next bit of information and then the interviewer would ask another question, essentially jumping into the space, creating a change of direction and erasing the final part of the story.

After two or three questions, I could feel a frustration in the situation, a mismatch. The actor was polite and played along to the end and reduced the amount of information in each corresponding answer. You do not want this to happen to you. You want the prospect to talk and give you as much information as possible. Information is power and the more you have it, the greater the chance you have of closing business.

The process we are discussing is the needs analysis phase of all sales communication. It doesn't matter if you are a telemarketer or new business sales person, the information should be gathered and recorded for current and future use. A prospect will move through a business is a structured way. The lead may be generated by a telemarketer, passed onto a new business sales consultant and onto a project delivery team and the corresponding needs analysis should move with them. I have seen this mistake so many times in the world of IT and I'm sure that it happens in so many others. The telemarketer will discuss with the client and a generated lead is passed to a person that visits them on site. The hand over was a simple discussion with no documentation. On site the sales person holds the conversation in greater detail and fills out the order form with an outline of the requirement. The project team deliver bespoke capability in the way that they feel is appropriate, often guided by their experiences of other customers.

Our needs analysis is designed to notate the most important things that the sale is going to solve, the needs. This is their expectation. As a company if you deliver, almost what they do want and some other stuff they didn't want you'll possibly find you are at some point dealing with a complaint, a situation to which your documentation doesn't correspond. To keep the customer happy, you end up doing work for free and the work that could have been sold as extras later has already been done so you lose out twice.

It doesn't hurt to have a crib sheet next to you to remind you of what to say if you enter a particular business area. If you sell, embroidery machines that create company logos on shirts, you need to understand the colour range they require. Is it black and white, tri-colour or pantone? What is the quality of the garments, silk, cotton or nylon? How large an area does the graphic need to cover? Is it button hole, breast pocket or the whole back of the shirt?

When I was initially trained in telemarketing, I bought tape programmes and books and many of them talked about the use of open and closed questions and although relevant at this stage don't get too hung up on the technicality of their use. An open question is a wonderful way to get someone to open up and tell you more, as long as you shut up and listen.

"Where do you see the company in five years?"

This is a fantastic use of a question. In this example the meaning the conscious mind associates is so vast that the prospect has to go inside and think of the answer. It isn't like that if you say:

"How many employees do you have?"

In this example they can instantly access that information and give an immediate reckoning. An open question is broad and wide and the information you get back in the answer may or may not help your cause.

At the early part of your conversation you want them to talk more than you talk to them. Have you ever been introduced to someone new and have later found out that they thought you were a nice guy or girl, even though in your mind you didn't say anything. When people speak about themselves and the passions they have in life, their hobbies, their children, maybe even the charities they are involved in, listening is the greatest rapport builder. This is high level rapport in action. You may not be a friend of theirs just yet, but may well be on the way to being a trusted advisor.

The closed question is where you confirm the detail. It may go something like this.

"So you said that you have lots of home workers and this was a bit of issue, how many exactly?"

I prefer to soften the start of the phrase as closed questions may easily appear to be an accusation. Take for example.

"Why do you have a bit of an issue with the home workers?"

You only need to hear children when they ask for something that is subsequently refused, the recurring 'why' is a word that you need to use sparingly. Be playful when you ask the prospect a question. Try not to appear guarded or needy. If you were face to face with someone you would nod to allow the prospects unconscious mind to accept that you are listening intently. We do the same with language, small verbal gestures that mark out a milestone of information and keep the prospect talking. They are hard to notate here, something like ah-hah or I see.

When you hear a natural pause or want to know more of the same, you can ask:

"What do you mean by that?"

On hearing this phrase the prospect will continue offering more detail. The role of the telemarketer is to listen. If you are the person asking all the questions and doing all the talking you don't have time to listen properly. In fact, you spend more time thinking of a clever question to use next, than you do processing the rich answer you have received and this is where you get mismatch. If your question doesn't fit in with the discussion you've been having, the prospect may pick up the smallest signal that you haven't been listening and rapport is lost. From that moment on, no amount of clever questioning is going to get you anywhere.

The best advice I can give you on asking a question is take real interest in the prospects business. Our problems begin when we assume we understand the business because we have sold to so many like them before. Wrong. All businesses are different. They perceive the world differently. They have a different take on the way the market is progressing for them. Some will be optimistic and some not so. Don't use your opinions to cloud their issues. Their world is a map that they understand. If they have an opinion you don't agree with, understand the reasoning behind it, you don't have to agree with them, but appreciation will go a long way in a business arrangement.

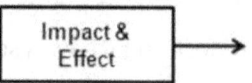

Impact & Effect. A great questioning technique reveals the business to you piece by piece. It adds clarity to your pre-work and assumptions. We can imagine all manner of things before we make the call and the reality is always different and surprising. The curiosity question opens the door and denotes a topic for you to explore. The open questions then probe the topic for more information with the finite detail coming from regimented closed questions.

So, what's missing from this formula?

Pain, pure and simple. It's okay knowing the inside leg measurement of a company, but this is not what's going to make you a sale. Your open questions may have found a few problems that the prospect has and now it's time to qualify if the problem warrants being pursued. In conversation with someone this happens all the time. Two colleagues that you interview separately may explain a situation using completely different words. What they are defining is similar, but the way words are used to express how they feel about the situation will often differ greatly. Say, for instance;

The salesperson: "I hear that there is a cold breeze that comes through the office window?"

Finance Director: "The air is freezing, I could hardly feel my hands and it's a nightmare."

Managing Director: "It does cause a draft, some people have complained."

If your company sells double glazing, it would be important now to find out if the business would warrant its time and money on repairing the situation. After all, if the managing director is using words like complained, it may not be on his prioritised radar. You see, our friend the finance director was empathic and used the word nightmare. Does this really mean it was a nightmare, more likely an overused word in his vocabulary?

You need to memorise three words, **effect**, **impact** and **consequence**. String a few sentences together and imagine the answers you get back.

- "What impact did that have on your business?"

- "When you complained to the boss about your cold hands, what effect did that have on him?"

- "If you don't fix that problem, what consequence do you think that will have?"

- "Will losing that order have wide ranging consequences?"

- "If your employees complain about a draft, will that have an effect on your decision?"

The answer will come back to you in one of two ways, either accepting that there is a need and the pain is large or that the topic you are describing is insignificant. If it's insignificant, strike the problem and probe a different area. If the pain is large, linger a while. Ask a few more questions.

- "What do you see as the solution?"

- "How quickly do you want to resolve it?"

- "If I could solve each of these things for you, what would be your priority?"

Whatever you do, don't start selling yet. At this stage in the conversation you have the prospect eating out of your hand. If they are open and the rapport is good, make sure that you have as much information as possible before looking to close. When the prospect suspects you are turning on the sales technique, it may be harder at a later stage to ask more questions and retain the same comfortable atmosphere.

When you've asked the questions using effect, impact and consequence make sure you allow the prospect to know that you have understood their answer. You can either, repeat their answer back to them turning the statement into a question, tell them that this is important and make a note or empathise with the current situation.

1. **Prospect:** "We have a real problem with drivers losing their mobile phones."

    Telemarketer: "You have a real problem with drivers losing their mobiles?"

2. **Prospect:** "We lost a customer because the quality of our yarn failed to meet their stringent standards?"

    Telemarketer: "Let me just make a note of that, that's important. What was the customer worth to you over the year?"

    A brilliant response. When you argue that your product or service is worth money, then the answer to these questions is where you hold the most leverage.

3. **Prospect:** "I get angry when I see the amount of money we lose."

    Telemarketer: "I can appreciate that. Who can afford to lose money, when it's so easy to do it properly?"

The moment the prospect accepts that they have a painful need and they offer information that quantifies its effect, you can capitalise on the information and proceed to close. You must and this is important, make accurate notes that reflect the prospects words. There is no point writing down, they have lost a few customers, when the prospect actually said we lost one customer last year and one this.

Paraphrasing the exact words is vitally important. It shows that you are a good listener. By matching the words you will remain in tight rapport. I mean by this, that your communication will remain at a higher level than just talk. The subconscious mind will forge strong ties, a congruent transport of ideas that will flow without critical thought getting in the way.

Whenever you meet someone or speak over the phone make good clear notes. With your imagination divide an A4 sheet of paper using four vertical lines and name them, problem, detail, operator and effect.

Prob	Detail	Op	Effect

As you ask questions problems or needs will arise, write a short description in the left hand column, for instance, windows are always dirty. Then with further questioning extract all of the detail surrounding that problem.

- The window cleaner should come on a Tuesday, but doesn't always arrive.
- Large Lorries on the road outside make the windows dirty very quickly.
- This is a show home and dirty windows doesn't look good to the clients.

The operator column refers to the people this problem affects. There is a subconscious communication here. People like to hear their name in conversation. It allows a connection at a deep level and aids the flow of rapport. When you ask the impactful questions, ie, questions that contain the words impact, effect or consequence you have actual people that will benefit from your proposed solution.

The conversation may go like this.

Telemarketer: "Whose office is facing the main road?"

Prospect: "The managing director's office is at the front along with the conference room."

Telemarketer: "The MD is that Shirley Lucas?"

Prospect: "Yes"

Finally, in the right hand column uncover the real pain by qualifying the need.   In actual fact, the information you gather in this column should almost equal the amount of information you have collected in the detail column. The more pain the client has, the greater the chance you have of closing the deal.

Prob	Detail	Op	Effect
The windows are always dirty			
	The window cleaner should come on a Tuesday, but doesn't always arrive		
	Large lorries on the road outside make the windows dirty very quickly		
	This is a show home and dirty windows doesn't look good to the clients		
		Joe and Mike	
			We lost two clients to the competitor
			Our company lost £2,000

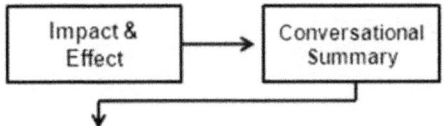

Conversational Summary. The conversational summary is a technique that works in all social and business interactions, either on the phone or face to face. At the end of a conversation with someone it is natural to say what you are going to do. Even if you've just had coffee with someone, you'll say "see you this time next week." It's natural to round up what a good time you've had with some rapport and then make another plan. Now in our social lives, these plans may be looser than in our business meetings. For instance, you may say "we must get together one night and have a meal." The intention is there, but the objective is not cemented.

The whole point of the business interaction is to achieve an objective. At this stage in the call you will have generated a list of information detailing the need and an accurate understanding of the pain behind it. Now is the time to let the prospect know that you have listened intently. If you have made accurate notes, this is easy. In much of your conversation this far, you have allowed the prospect to be in control, allowing them to respond to open questions. As you've needed clarity you've asked closed questions to gain the detail. This is the time for you to take control. Use words that round up and prioritise and aim to get the prospect to agree with your summary. Something like this:

Prospect: "Yes, we find the smaller mower very time consuming and the lawns don't look as good as they should to the general public?"

(Pain)

Telemarketer: "What effect does that have on your ticket prices?" (Impactful question)

Prospect: "I can't be sure, but I'm pretty sure those that visit wouldn't come back any time soon?"

(Pain explained at a deeper level)

Telemarketer: "What percentage of people would you like to come back?"

(Closed question to gather information for return on investment)

Prospect: "I want at least 50% of people to come back in the year, at the moment this is only 10% or so."

(You now have all of the information you need to create a compelling case)

Telemarketer: "Can we just stop there a moment, I want to make sure that I have this down correctly, is that okay?"

(The conversational summary temporarily halts proceedings)

Prospect: "Fine."

Telemarketer: "So, in terms of the gardens you want to get another 40% of people back through the gate, that's quite a figure."

(Listen for subconscious agreement like uh-huh).

"And the main culprit for this is the lawns that don't look as good as they should do."

(This is spoken as if you are pondering the theory of life and relativity giving the impression that you are deeply involved in helping to solve the problem)

"I see, so it's pretty important to get the mower speed increased. What solutions have you looked at, to solve this?"

(Digging to see what competition you are up against, remember SCOTSMAN).

Prospect: "I've been too busy to consider all of the products on the market?"

You can see where the discussion is going. The prospect is going to ask you about a solution, especially if they don't perceive you as a threat or an in the face sales person. Hold off making a recommendation as long as possible, with more information, the more chance you have of building buyer potential.

In cases where there has been more than one need discovered, a conversational summary should prioritise the needs before delivering any solutions. You may have found that the untidy lawns were one problem. The gravel on the drive doesn't match the strong white patterns of the brickwork and maybe the paintwork on the orangery is looking less than crisp and clean, all perfectly reasonable problems for a business to want to solve. You may well have a one solution that fits all of these problems and can proceed accordingly, but it is worth checking what firm ideas the prospect has.

- Do you have a plan of attack?
- Which of these is the most important?
- Are you going to hit all of these at one go or prioritise?
- Does the mower need your attention first or the gravel on the drive?

These questions will give you all you need, the reasons why and any information such as compelling events. You are almost there.

Sell the Close

Sell the Close. So here we are, finally in the zone and ready to speak about our products and services. As you've picked your way through the detail of the prospects individual need you'll have been matching the responses to a solution that you can offer. This doesn't always happen, sometimes you have no answer or your products aren't an appropriate match. Be sure before you close the call that you are sure you have conducted a full needs analysis though and you have understood the requirement properly. If you don't have a solution (SCOTSMAN) it is better to be honest and step away from the deal rather than to waste more time.

If you have a solution, be sure to deliver your idea precisely and simply. You may want to test the water before jumping in with both feet. If you make the mistake of giving your solution to the need in one hit you may run the risk of receiving opposition to your idea.

"We've tried that before", or "I've considered that approach and it won't work for us because…" are all possibilities. Test by softening your question.

- I have an idea that might interest you
- Have you ever considered…?
- I have a customer that…(the My Friend John technique. By talking about another company, relaying their story. A usual way to disassociate meaning and test for suitability)
- I suppose you've considered…
- There's a number of ways that you might consider…
- I have an idea I can bring to the table…

Keep your idea short and check that the prospect is following you, although it is your time to speak, listen for the clues that the prospect is still on board. In the next section we'll be looking at how you can handle the objections that will come up. Importantly objections are only questions. Human beings only ask questions if they want to know more, handle them properly.

At the end of the day you are there to achieve an objective such as, ask for the order, set a meeting date or schedule another call. Again, this is another task in the role of the telemarketer that you can plan ahead of time. In so many training sessions with sales people young and old I ask the question, "Who is afraid of asking for the order?" and the hands go up.

The closing question strikes fear into even the most competent of sales people. Why, do you ask? It's not difficult, it's just another question and you're exactly right. It is just another question. Bide by the rules and it will all go well.

1. Prepare and be comfortable with your closing question, practise it out loud ahead of time.

2. Deliver the closing question with congruency.

3. Be quiet. He who speaks first has lost.

Generally, one closing question is all you need to get by in sales. Find one that suits you style. It doesn't need to be long or too wordy. It needs to roll out of your mouth nonchalantly at the right time. Try a few of these and create your own.

- Do you want it then?

- What do you think?

- I could have that on site in time for the weekend?

- I've got this model in black or the blue if you prefer?

- Tell you what, shall I get my technical director, Bob to come in and get the ball rolling?

Every sales book on the planet will give you hundreds of examples of how to close. Think of it this way, the hard work has all been done, this question is the culmination of all of your professionalism over the phone. You deserve to get the order.

Deliver the message congruently. The subconscious mind can easily identify if the way you are speaking fails to match your deeply held desire. As a professional telemarketer you are there to help the prospect achieve more. If you whole heartedly believe you are there to help the prospect achieve the greater good then your body language and vocal patterns will support your beliefs. If the prospect spends some substantial time on the telephone talking to you, I can guarantee they are only still there because the rapport you have is serving to convince them that your intentions are honourable. By practising the question out loud before you make the call you will iron out the apprehension, the erms, the stutter and the additional breaths. Say it over and over and over. When you're in front of the prospect, carefully drop the question into the conversation at the appropriate time and the results will surprise you.

When you have delivered the closing question, be quiet. The psychology of the moment is simple. When you ask the question the prospect has to take their thoughts internally to think. They add up all of the things you've said and manually build pathways linking everything together. It's the crux moment. We all do it just before we buy, we ponder. Should we, shouldn't we. By staying quiet you are allowing this to happen naturally.

Want to know how to blow the sale?

Start talking. If you talk while they are thinking, it stops the sales process and you have to go back and build again. You are slowly talking the prospect out of the sale. This stupidity is called oversell. Take yourself back a while to when you were a complete novice and you decided that telemarketing was the profession for you. You joined a company and worked hard, learnt the ropes, bought a couple of audio courses to listen to and built your skills to a professional level. In this one call you have got it all perfectly right and the goal is within sight and then you ask the closing question and talk. All that hard work for nothing.

When you ask the question, sit quietly and listen. It should be so silent that you cannot hear anything at all. No rustling paper, no conversations with others in the office nothing. You may hear um's and ah's that's great. Be prepared for those prospects that are sitting on the fence, they may take minutes, don't talk until you are spoken to. You may be asked to make assurances, to set their mind at ease on a couple of important points. Answer and then be quiet again.

When the client says yes, act responsibly. Be polite and state the next steps. The forms to be signed, the credit check, the payment by credit card, etc. Don't rejoice and shout yippee or you will invoke an early form of buyers remorse.

State what you are going to do and when and stick to your promises. Follow up with email confirmations of the documents and make sure you include, welcome on board. This is one of the only times you want to use email. It is so impersonal and so easily misconstrued. If you have important information always ring your new customer. These calls help you build even greater rapport and a business relationship and fend off any misgivings or buyers remorse.

The Magic Story
There are lots of great ways to get your message across, always strive for brevity and clarity. The prospect doesn't want or need too much detail just enough to make the decision. Detail overload can easily stall the sale.

First of all, think of a way of explaining your product or service in an exciting way. Sounds simple doesn't it, but many presentations over the phone sound decidedly boring. The main technique here is to be passionate about what you do and who you are. It's that congruency thing again. Your words have to match your intentions and if they don't the prospect will never buy into your story.

Take this as an example. You sell drinking water. Granted, not the most exciting of products in the world, but true telemarketers will spin a web of intrigue and sell the dream. This is not just water. This is rain water that fell over a thousand years ago, filtered through underground rocks of the Appalachia's and pumped directly out to the still with nothing added, without doubt the purest drinking experience in the World today.

Or this. Milk and butter, from Jersey cows that spend all year luxuriating in the warm hills of the Dunstable Downs, eating the finest rye grass. This milk is so special that it's only used in products that require a richer, iron content. Quality reserved for only the finest products from our diary.

Pick out the finer points and elaborate on them, tell a fascinating story. Don't lie and I emphasis this, don't tell lies about your product. There are so many things you can say about the simplest of products, just think of the potential when you have more complex solutions. Get used to the story. Share it with your colleagues. You only need 30 seconds or so to stake your claim.

The way you build a story is by using a simple formula, known in sales as FAB, features, advantages and benefits. In many ways we are all adept at knowing what we do. As a business owner you've created a product that you are passionate about, spent years in research and development and know every nook and cranny of its brilliance. Now here's the thing, you need to sell the concept to the outside world. There are a few ways you can do this. You may choose to let some important people have the product on trial. This is an interesting method, they get to see first hand what the product will do, but does it work? Not often. Until a prospect actually sees some value in what the item will do for them, it is unlikely it will be tried and tested.

As a young account manager so many resellers would ask me for demonstration product to supply to their prospects believing that if only they would get their hands on it, they would see the value and instantly purchase. In the majority of cases it didn't work. Thinking about SCOTSMAN again, the authority is the person that can make the decision, right? They have the power to spend the money and make the decision. I am assuming that your product would be tested by them, certainly in larger companies this is not the case. A technical person would take the product on board and give it the once over. What chance has the technical person got of relaying your products features to the person that can make the decision, using your magic story and impressing how the product will save money and time in the business? In most cases, the decision has been made before you even get the chance to discuss your ideas.

The other thing is that good companies are busy and great companies are even busier. When you deliver your product without the chance of an introduction it is easy for them to say give me a free trial, but where is their commitment and priority? With so many things on the go, how will they ever put your product first and get on and use it. In reality, they never do. In 30 days you are asked to extend the trial and spend a great deal of time chasing them, almost to the point where they have forgotten why they were interested in the first place.

At the early stage of the sale, use FAB - features, advantages and benefits to gauge the interest of the prospect before making any financial commitments on your part. By turning initial interest into desire, you will have the opportunity to assess real interest over passive involvement. The tyre kicker is always around to waste your time and energy, but don't make the mistake of creating a poor sales situation and pursuing the wrong target.

The features, you already know. These are the things you have built into you product or service which make it usable or unique. If you are a window cleaner working in the corporate market you might boast that 95% of your work is done before the shops open for business. This might be a great selling feature, but listen to it from a prospects point of view.

"95% of our work is done before the shops open!"

Listening as the prospect, this phrase doesn't intrigue or inspire me. It doesn't set me alight. It doesn't make me want to change my window cleaner, right now. So, we need to add some additional words that quantify what the service will give to them.

"95% of our work is done before the shops open, which means that your retail clients will only ever see the results of our labour, not workmen obstructing the view."

Now, we are getting somewhere. The additional sentence builds on the first and explains the advantages of using you, the window cleaner. This is correct, but you haven't quite achieved the objective. I can still hear the words, 'so what' emanating from the prospects thoughts. If you can use the phrase 'so what' at the end of a sales pitch then you haven't hit the mark. You may have been in danger of listings loads of features and the decision maker is saying inside his head, "so what, what's in it for me". There has to be a 'what's in it for me', or they won't buy. Remember, the majority of prospects buying products do so because they have a need. Let's finish our sentence.

"95% of our work is done before the shops open, which means that your retail clients will only ever see the results of our labour, not workmen obstructing the view. Our cleaning service ensures that your customers always see a clean establishment and view your products at the best quality in town. I'm sure that will bring in more sales."

The benefit of your proposition is what it's all about. As a buyer I'm not interested in how many widgets a thing has, or how shiny the paint is, I want to know what it will do for me. When you are explaining your value proposition in the early stages of the conversation, you can offer wide and varied examples. Whereas later in the conversation, you'll want to use examples that satisfy the individual needs you have uncovered. This is the ultimate way to close a sale. Know what and when to sell your ideas and know when to stop talking. Don't oversell. By talking about all the features that the product or service has will simply overload the imagination of the buyer. It is far better to leave them wanting more, than confusing them to such a state that it all seems too complicated to use or implement.

Here's another example:

Feature: "Our cupcakes are made from organic ingredients only."

Advantage: "We can personally guarantee the source of each natural component which means that the product is consistent in taste, time after time."

('Which means that' is a useful linguistic bridge.)

Benefit: "Natural ingredients always have the best taste, work well for people with special dietary requirements and are better for your health."

A few more examples:

"As you'll discover this camera has a fully automatic lens cover (feature), which protects the optical parts (advantage). You'll never have to worry about sand damage when you take this item to the beach." (benefit)

"We've been in the business rates market for over thirty years, rest assured we've dealt with your specific billing council and can use that experience to get you the best possible deal."

"We're one of the few firework companies that trade all the year round. It doesn't matter if you have a birthday party or wedding reception, we can supply products that are right for you all year round. We'll make it an extra special occasion."

"Our rooms at the hotel are designed for the professional travelling businessman. Free internet access, areas for break outs and business meetings, great food and a productivity package which means that you can conduct all of your meetings without travelling too far. Our flexibility will help save you money by seeing more customers in one place."

It doesn't matter what you do as a business, build your message in order. This is what you do (a feature of your product or service), what it will give them (an advantage of the feature) and the real reason they should buy (the benefit). If this benefit matches their need you have the opportunity to close.

Guarantee
Everyone likes a guarantee when buying a product. The basic term of money back or quality assured overcomes one of the fundamental objections or stalling points which invoke buyer's remorse, "What if I don't like it" or "The product doesn't work for me."

When we consider a product our brains are attempting to objectively assess if this is right for us. The telemarketer in the conversation is using techniques to help the prospect make the right choice and that is important. If you railroad the person into making a purchase even though it isn't right for them, the chances of buyer's remorse will increase exponentially and may eventually lead to an unsatisfied customer. These types of transactions do little to build the brand and run the risk of a long term detrimental effect on the business.

At the right time in the sales process introducing a guarantee is a useful turning point in the decision making process. Here is an example of how a MLM- multi-level marketing company quantifies a guarantee to its distributors.

"We are so convinced that you will not only like, but adore our products and reseller programme that we offer this guarantee. If you are not 100% satisfied by the end of the first year, you can resign your position and the company will refund the cost of membership in full and buy back all of the unopened products you have remaining. We do this to give you the opportunity to see first hand exactly how the business works and the profits that can be made. With over 10,000 home resellers in this country, we wouldn't be in business if we hadn't got it right."

Of course, the words can be delivered in a million different ways, but the sentiment behind them is the same. There is no risk, give it a go. If you don't like it, we take it back, it doesn't cost you anything. In reality, if you have great products or service that you stand by, returns will be minimal and your list of satisfied customers will grow.

How many times have you seen presentations on the television for items such as steam mops, kitchen equipment, weight loss products and all of them have either a 30 day or 60 day money back, no quibble guarantee. After giving the details of the product and case studies of how their customers have benefited from this service, the symbol for the guarantee is shown. It wraps up an impressive presentation followed by the prices.

Now, you might be thinking right now that this won't work for me because...and the list of reasons will be flooding from your mouth. Let's look at a few examples.

- I sell fish and chips and my customers would all eat for free

- We are in a service industry and we sell time. When the time has gone, we cannot recoup the loss

- I resell a product and the manufacturer will not guarantee its quality to me, so my company would lose out

- I am scared that the returns would be so high that financially it would be unsustainable.

These are all valid and well thought out reasons to not give a guarantee. Especially when your business is small it would be foolish to make financial claims you cannot stand by, but it doesn't stop you from using the technique. You can still make claims that are true.

- "We only use sustainable fish from well managed and guaranteed sources."

- "Our price is individually calculated on each project and includes the installation and 1st year's maintenance."

- "This product received the Seal of Quality Approved award in 2013 for its outstanding build quality."

- "We personally guarantee that only engineers with this qualification will conduct the work."

- "Our cleaners are all regularly checked by the criminal records bureau and have licences to work on education premises."

A guarantee can easily reflect your unique selling point or contain a summary of your business value proposition. We looked at these earlier. When you deliver your guarantee over the phone wait until the prospect is thinking about making a purchase, right at the moment when they begin to go inside and think of all of the benefits, deliver the guarantee. Speak confidently. This is another thing that you can practise ahead of time.

Pricing your product or service

There is a specific psychology you really should consider before confirming and advertising your prices.   We all know there are luxury and budget products out there, some that attract a premium mark up, whereas others make up the business revenue by enormous amounts of small purchases. Where does your proposition sit?

If you cannot differentiate what you do in the marketplace or industry, how will you expect the prospect to pay more for what you do?

Say for instance, you have created a web site to sell printer consumables for every make and model on the market. The web site has an e-commerce front end and shows a small cost for delivery. What is the differentiation? You can buy printer cartridges from shops on the high street and a multitude of web sites, so why would I buy from you?

- Can you claim your delivery is exceptionally fast?

- That you sell a printer cartridge that lasts a whole lot longer than any others on the market?

- That you have in stock toner cartridges for older, out of date models?

- You have an angle where your production and delivery process is so much greener due to recycling?

- You have a system where each purchase accrues points and these can exchanged for prizes or other services?

Without a tick against any of these or similar ideas, you are saying to the prospect, "Look on the internet and buy the cheapest you can find!" You will have an up hill battle trying to convince a prospect of your ideas.

I have a friend that sells high quality Christmas baubles on the internet. Hand crafted that retail for as little as £25 each. The phrase 'little as' may raise eyebrows from some of you reading this. If you have absolutely no interest in Christmas or the paraphernalia surrounding it then £25 might seem an incredible amount of money, but by operating in this niche market there are buyers that will pay many times more for this type of speciality. Consider the value proposition in this marketplace.

- Each item is handcrafted and unique, the buyer has the only copy

- Christmas decorations of this quality last for years , they are timeless and can be handed down the generations of families

- They make ideal Christmas gifts that cannot be purchased anywhere else

- The value of these items will continue to increase, year on year

Whether it's a niche market or more horizontal in nature, you will have considered the opportunity when you set the business up, now is the time to capitalise on the value proposition and set the price accordingly. If the prices are high you have the opportunity to negotiate with your prospects to motivate the sale, if the prices are low this may not be an option. Rewarding regular purchases is a popular way to reward loyalty and build your brand.

Up-front Preparation

Preparation

In earlier chapters, I have impressed the need for preparation. In fact, so much of the role of the professional telemarketer can be pre-rehearsed and this is what sets you head and shoulders above all of the others making calls. This is where technique wins the day and increases your chances of making sale.

As I've said before the conversation must not be scripted or the prospect will identify the poor quality of communication subconsciously. You won't sound like you're a professional or someone to be trusted, more a hired hand in a poorly paid telesales role. Professional telemarketing people are more than this. They are an intrinsic cog in the success of any sales orientated company and generate invaluable new business contacts that can be quantified and measured. With this preparation you are already 35% more likely to close business.

The Murder Bag

I came across this term when speaking to a double glazing salesman in the 90's. We were discussing the sales approach he used when calling door to door and murder bag came out in the conversation. A murder bag is a kit of everything you need to achieve your objective on the call. You don't want to leave the prospect and return two days later with direct debit forms or produce a detailed proposal. You simply call on the murder bag to close the sale at the appropriate moment. In the world of double glazing the murder bag contained.

- Samples of the different coloured plastics used at the time

- Laminated pictures of the variety of fixings and handles on offer

- A price list

- Printed contracts

- Case studies

- Brochures

In the role of professional telemarketer you should do the same. Have to hand all of the things you need in the course of your conversations.

- A diary for booking appointments

- A form to collect additional information

- A price list

- A note pad to write down objections you were unable to overcome

- An email system to confirm details to the prospect

Diary. The diary may be electronic in the form of Microsoft Outlook or paper based, it doesn't really matter. Just make sure that when you discuss when and where you can easily read and append as necessary. Once or twice I've seen diaries in hairdressers or garages which have been impossible to read quickly and the last thing you want is to call them back to change the appointment after a mistake. In Outlook, a company diary can also be confusing. When you have multiple sales people on one page, it may not be immediately clear, especially when you have the stress of closing before the call ends. Keep on top of the diary and don't make promises you can't keep. At this point, we can also mention the SmartPhone. A diary on a small device such as this is often cumbersome and takes a few seconds more to navigate than its paper based equivalent. Whichever method you use just remember the prospect wants to book quickly and be sent a reminder, don't make this a long session of erm's and indecisiveness. Make the appointment and move on.

Additional Information. A needs analysis form is a handy tool even if you know the industry inside out. The form, ideally no more than one side of A4 is a statement of affairs for this prospect. It shows the types of products and services you sell and the needs you've uncovered. If there are things you need to know before a sale can take place then make sure they are on the form, use it as a checklist. We spoke earlier about SCOTSMAN and the power it has to qualify a prospect for your product. Tick the items off as you satisfy yourself that your product or service is right for the prospect.

Prices. A price list is pretty fundamental. If someone is interested in your products they will want to know how much. Don't be apologetic about the price when you deliver it. You may lose sales from time to time based on price, make a note of the occasion and use it for review later on. You will often notice companies quoting by the hour or week instead of a total figure. It sounds so much cheaper if you say just £2 a day instead of £735 a year. Insurance is often sold like this, especially when you give the prospect the option to buy using a monthly direct debit.

This section of the book is all about preparation. When you start calling for the first time the calls will throw up all manner of objections and questions that you simply cannot respond to. Make a note of them and then work the revised answers into your scripts.

The benefits of CRM – Customer Relationship Management software
Data is a valuable commodity in business. Whether you buy your calling list or build it over time, it is easy to understand why you need to protect it. In the early years of my sales career we would have an A4 sheet of paper for each prospect and write a line for each conversation we would have along with the date and time. If the prospect would tell me to call back I would write a number on the top for filing, say 2/12, 2nd week of December. A simple, cost free and effective way of storing possibilities. However if you are serious about building long term relationships you may need more features.

- Password and security controlled. With multiple sales people in your organisation you may want some records hidden or at least that the entire database cannot be stolen in one hit. One of the worries of sales people is that they may leave and join a competitor.

- A reminder system that links in with your diary of choice. As your database grows, so will the number of call backs you will set against each record. A prospect may say "Call me back in the quiet period over Christmas" or "Wait until my accounts are done at year end." As a telemarketer you will be responsible for ensuring that not only calls to new businesses take place, but the existing customers you have are serviced correctly.

- Link documents to CRM. Your communications will be a mixture of telephone calls, emails sent / received and face-to-face meetings. By attaching all of the documents and presentations that you send and receive you will always have a complete overview of what has been discussed.

- Send email marketing. In the first chapter we spoke about the power of collaborative marketing and how calling warm leads is far more effective than cold calling. Many software packages will send emails promoting your products and report back click and open information in conjunction with your web site. Not only can you call from a list of interested people, you can also produce useful statistics on what campaigns really work.

These are just a few of the features that a CRM software package will offer you. These are available in many formats, for all sizes of business. You may want to consider the options of buying and running the software on your local machine or renting the package and connecting via the internet. You may just need it on the desktop computer next to your desk phone or combined with a SmartPhone for mobile use.

Finding the Motivation

To find the motivation to succeed, you have to have an end goal, an objective. If you work for someone as a telemarketer, ask yourself, what is the salary and commission you want to make this month? If it's your business, what turnover and profitability do you need to achieve to satisfy the business plan?

Break the target down into what you need to do today along with the sales ratio we spoke about in the earlier chapter. Set your stall out the night before, know who you are going to call and have your murder bag on the desk. Get in the office 10 minutes early and be ready to hit the phones as soon as offices open.

Get rid of as many distractions as you can. If you're working from home, move that TV, turn off the mobile phone and close your web browser. Don't touch any of these things for at least 90 minutes until you have a chunk of the calling done. Keep the phone in your hand constantly so no one can put calls through to you. Avoid the office banter and gossip. You'll hear it all again later anyway.

Be clear in your mind how much every call means to your success. If you can calculate that every missed call is costing you £5, it wouldn't take you long to realise, success comes from achieving the numbers.

Now, attitude. Many sales people think that telemarketing is not the best use of their time and when they are told to call migrate away to something else they like doing. In fact, they use all the excuses in the world to avoid picking up the phone. Remember this point. Calling on the telephone is the easiest way to spend your life. Change your attitude towards calling. How easy can it be? You have a list of calls to make. A list of little conversations where the answer is either yes or no and that is it. You don't have anyone complaining at you, chasing you for quotes, dragging you into other tasks that have nothing to do with you, because your head is down and they cannot distract you if the phone is in your hand. You don't even have to make a round of drinks. Your colleagues will make them for you.

Telemarketing is simple if you follow the techniques outlined in this book. To achieve massive success in telemarketing you need to be consistent and hit the numbers you have laid out. Like I said before, record what you have done in terms of effort, number of calls, the decision makers you've spoken to and the number of appointments or sales you've made. The moment your first sale comes in, you will realise the importance of becoming a professional, not just a person that has been forced into calling because you have to.

Getting past the gatekeeper
First of all, what is a gatekeeper?

Companies don't set out to employ people to make the life of the telemarketer difficult. Gatekeepers are anyone that asks questions before putting the call through to the decision maker. They may ask:

- "Can I ask what it's regarding?"

- "Have you spoken to him/her before?"

Gatekeepers, often the receptionist of the business are astute people that want to act professionally in the eyes of their boss. You can see from their point of view that putting every cold call through to a director may cause them an amount of embarrassment. Gatekeepers like to develop a reason for accepting the call and will announce you accordingly.

There are two ways to prepare. The simpler option is to change the time of your call. If the gatekeeper is in residence every day from 9am to 5pm, make a note in CRM in your activity notes to find out times when they are not on site. Most people take a lunch hour, test call between midday and 2pm. I am often surprised how many managing directors answer the switchboard before 9am before most employees even make it into work.

The second method to overcome the gatekeeper is to use language to eliminate their fears that you are simply making a cold call. Prepare fashioned responses to the gatekeeper questions, remembering to keep your answer within context. What I mean by that is, don't lie. Nothing will be worse than the gatekeeper putting you through and the decision maker has no idea who you are. In response to:

"Can I ask what it's regarding?'"

"I am following up an email I sent her offering language classes last week."

This doesn't sound like a concrete reason for you to be put through. The meaning is more speculative in nature.

"Can you tell her Ian Thompson is calling regarding property insurance please."

The front part of this sentence has a strange effect on our senses. By using our name we instantly sound familiar. By delivering our name we are creating a presupposition that a previous contact has taken place. However, the second half of the sentence is weak. You can assume a gatekeeper is the type of person that will have a wider knowledge of the organisation and they instantly will respond with a negative reflex response. Such as "We already have insurance" from then on your road to successful contact will have been thwarted.

I am of course assuming that this is the first call to this company and your decision maker. The technique of putting the name first would work really well if you were to add:

"It's Ian Thompson of Agra Insurance, she asked me to call again today."

Let's try another example attempting to be less vague about our purpose.

"Can you tell her Ian Thompson is calling, I have some information on competitive insurance on these properties."

We could also invoke the referral technique.

"Could you tell her Ian Thompson is calling, I've been working with Emphasis Design next door to you on a project she might find interesting."

Notice how this comment is the same as our curiosity question, you can't help as a prospect to want to know more. The gatekeeper is likely to ask "What project is that?"

From here, you will need to tread carefully. If you say insurance you may open up to the negative reflex response once more, "We have insurance."

You may infer that confidentiality agreements are in place or that you need to clarify a few points before offering the full information. It may not be appropriate to give confidential information to anyone except the directors of the business. Be tactful and not demeaning.

"I appreciate all of the buildings on this estate are insured, Emphasis Design were exactly the same, we've made some important changes that have reduced costs in regards to their policy, it might be of interest to Mr Stapleton, do you mind putting me through."

Rarely will a gatekeeper continue with more than two questions, they simply don't have the time. If you've supplied a compelling argument, you will get through. On the odd occasion you don't get through, be polite and leave the call.

"Have you spoken to her before?"

This is a great question on the part of the gatekeeper. If you say no, you find the negative reflex response again, "Send her something in the post" or "She doesn't take cold calls." If you say yes, you are breaking your moral code and stand the chance of sounding like a liar if you get through to her. Taking each of these on face value, imagine the response you will get from the gatekeeper.

"I spoke to Mary back in September and she indicated the business reviewed insurance before the start of the year."

In this sentence I have used her forename, Mary. Telemarketing in general, is becoming less formal and attitudes to the surname only approach have changed. Gauge your decision maker in terms of age and situation and act appropriately. The rest of the sentence isn't a strong approach. You can almost feel the negative reflex response about to happen.

"We already have that covered."

"I haven't spoken to Mary before, Mrs Kemble of Wright Brothers said she would introduce my name when they next meet."

Building reference and referral potential makes your life a whole lot easier. When you do good work for someone ask them to refer you to someone they know and follow it up. This is free marketing.

"We are both members of the Business Networking Group in Birmingham, can she spare me a few minutes?"

Make sure you are a member of the group before you use this. Most of the business groups you can join will give you the contact names of other members either at launch parties, luncheons or in their magazine. Companies attend these functions to network and this is how you will be perceived. You may want to get to know the decision maker better before trying to sell them your products or services.

"I am looking to invite financial directors to a business event we are running in September, can Mrs Wainwright spare me a few minutes?" Which particular director or decision maker does your product most appeal to? Say it's the finance director because your company sell energy, gas and electric. Start the conversation off by saying we are holding an event in Coventry (or place local to them) which is going to discuss the impact of energy prices on the SME (small & medium enterprise), would you be interested in attending this type of thing? Whatever they say, it is easy for you to slip in the conversation:

"Who are your main suppliers at the moment?'

One last thought. Treat the gatekeeper with respect. They often hold the keys to a substantial amount of trust in the organisation. It is better for you to be forgotten than remembered for all the wrong reasons.

Voicemail

Most telephone systems have voicemail attendants and these prove to be useful electronic versions of the gatekeeper. The notes you make in CRM are important here. I wouldn't normally leave a message if I were greeted by voicemail until I was able to build a pattern of the person I was calling. With each call I make, I enter a short reason why I didn't get through. It might be, voicemail, nml (no message left), not in the office today, not at his desk, no answer on his extension, colleague took a message etc. It's useful to record this information as well as the date and the time of the call.

Why do I record the pattern?

The pattern of answers can give you an indication of the type of company and person you are talking to. If they are varied with each call, a mixture of not at his desk, on the phone or in a meeting, you can begin to realise that this is the person you want to speak to. They are busy, running around with a million plates spinning in the air. Whereas a continuous list of voicemails, may mean that this person uses voicemail as a way of filtering calls from the outside world and you may feel helpless to respond to this stonewall attitude.

Well, don't despair, everyone has a way of communicating and finding out about the things that they want or need. Here are a few ways to stimulate the minds of those that remain elusive.

- Leave a well scripted voicemail

- Speak to a colleague to find out more about the decision maker

- Invite to an event that includes other decision makers and members of their peer group

- Find a company that deal with your prospect and ask for a referral

Consider all of your options before leaving a voicemail. Leaving voicemail is a widely speculative event that requires a large amount of unqualified mind reading. In most cases you have never spoken to this person and will assume certain aspects of what they do and how they like to operate, this is a dangerous pastime.

If the message you leave is misunderstood and memorable you run the risk of alienating the relationship before it has even begun. Return to the curiosity question we studied in an earlier chapter. Can you create a level of intrigue that prompts an interested person to call you back? The answer is, if the decision maker makes a point of not using the telephone as a primary source of communication you are probably making it hard for yourself. In collaborative marketing, we use a multitude of methods to drive interest through our central portal the web site. An emailed newsletter might entice a reader to see examples of your work on the web site, a telesales call may be used to introduce decision makers to new concepts and a range of videos on YouTube and printed postcards may educate team members by advertising events on the home page.

What stops you from using the same technique?

Voicemail: "Stephanie Harris is not here right now. If you'd like to leave a message speak after the bleep."

Telemarketer: "Good morning Ms Harris, I trust you are well. My name is Alex Smith, I was hoping to catch you in the office today. My company, Vision Design & Printing are having a launch evening at the Guildhall in May. The details are posted at www.vision.co.uk. We hope to see you there."

In this example, I've kept the words specifically short. Don't ramble. Try to leave a message that they don't have to replay over and over to get the number. In this case, what we do is obvious we sound exactly like a Print and Copy Company. If the name of your business is generic, craft a message that says what you do. The venue is also an interesting hook line. If you say the Hotel on Coventry Road, it sounds like another room with no view. Yet the Guildhall, the art gallery, the museum, the secret bunker, the stately home, all places you can rent reasonably cheaply nowadays will attract more people to look at the web site. When it comes to the web address, keep it short and memorable, trying to listen to a sub page on an answer machine is very tedious and never reliable. Send the decision maker to your home page and ensure it contains a big banner or splash directing them to the event.

Here's another.

Voicemail: "Leave a message after the beep."

Telemarketer: "Ms Harris, Alex Smith of Vision Design and Print. I wanted to make contact as I've been working with your neighbour, Alamanac over the last few months, you may have noticed their new brand and signage. I wondered if a design refresh was something you may consider. If it's of interest, take a look our work at www.visiondp.co.uk, that's www.v-i-s-i-o-n-d-p.co.uk. Thanks for your time."

Still using the web site as a central point, this message is short and clear. There is nothing stopping you from dropping examples of the work in an envelope as a reminder. People won't necessarily notice signage immediately until it is pointed out to them. When it finally meets their conscious awareness, they will put two and two together.

At the end of the voicemail, I've repeated the web address, said slowly this allows the decision maker to make a note of the address without repeating the message. Make it as simple as possible to do business with you.

Voicemail: "I am away from my desk or in a meeting, leave a message."

Telemarketer: "This is a message for Ms Stephanie Harris. My name is Alex Smith of Vision Printing, we're doing some great work for a company on the Parkhill Industrial Estate at the moment and I was hoping to catch a few minutes of your time. Do you think you could call me on 07987 888XXX, that's 07987 888XXX."

This works if the Parkhill Estate has some businesses the others in the area aspire to be or if the prospects competitor resides there. It is always worth impressing that time is valuable.

No call is wasted if you can find out more about the person or business you are calling about. If a colleague tells you that the person you want is on holiday for example you can rebuttal with:

"Does Mike still deal with new suppliers?"

In fact, if you word the question correctly any gaps in your needs analysis can be collected.

If you sell catering services your needs analysis I'm sure would include the number of full time employees on site and whether the facility offered supplemented meals to its staff. In the conversation you discover this information even without getting through to the decision maker.

Telemarketer: "Can I speak to Neil Andrews please?"

Colleague: "I'm sorry he isn't in the office today."

Telemarketer: "I wanted to drop Neil an invite to a launch party on venue catering services, I'll do that by email. Before I go, there were a couple of details I needed to confirm, can you help?"

Colleague: "Sure."

Telemarketer: "I've been asked to collect some information for demographics, the number of employees and whether the company has an on site canteen, is that okay?"

The words 'can you help' disarm most of us. In fact, we go out of our way to be friendly and offer all sorts of information when asked, especially when the questions don't affect us personally. Many a tight negotiation has been foiled when information vital to the deal has already been discovered from third party sources within the business. The only caveat is if the person is reluctant. Simply say:

"I fully understand. I will speak to him directly."

If you haven't managed to speak to the decision maker then you want the others in the office to forget your company and you. The last thing you want is the decision maker to hear that you have hounded a receptionist monotonously and made a nuisance of yourself.

The Instant Negative Reaction Response
This is a phenomenon that happens almost by accident. The caller instantly triggers the critical thought of the gatekeeper and a phrase is

instantly fired in response to your question. There is little substance to the response, but it leaves the telemarketer stumped and unable to repose skilfully.

Say you have introduced yourself and asked to speak to the decision maker. The gatekeeper responds with "What's it regarding?" and you say:

"I wanted to discuss the cost of telephone calls with her."

The gatekeeper will respond with "We already have someone that deals with that" or "We have that covered" or "We signed a contract last week."

- "I'm not interested."

- "We're taken care of."

- "Stick something in the post"

Without preparation it is impossible to respond with sufficient quality to overcome the blockage. A good gatekeeper is somewhat of a master at delivering phrases which remove your positive approach and unhinge expectation. The answer is to make a note of all of the negative reaction responses you can imagine and create working patterns to get you past the gatekeeper.

Before you craft elegant responses, scrutinise your curiosity questions to ensure you aren't needlessly generating these answers. Prevention is always better than the cure in this case.

Send me some information in the post
"It would be my pleasure to send you some information. The only problem is, there are so many things I could send. Do you mind if I ask you a few questions to see what's most appropriate for you?"

I'm not interested
"I didn't expect you to be interested immediately, business owners always need to hear the facts before that happens. Can I clarify a few points with you?"

We signed a contract last week
"I'm glad to hear you take this area of your business seriously, many don't. I've asked this question of so many owners and found that the product we offer meets so many more needs. Do you mind if we look at some comparisons for your next review?"

There are lots of examples on the internet of how to overcome all manner of verbal misdirection. This is not what I want to offer you. Get used to writing your own examples that match your talking style.
When you read them out loud, you express a style that is specific to you and the context of what you are selling. That means that the examples you create will develop over time with usage and change with each style of call you make. A telemarketer is far more flexible if they are able to pick up on the type of misdirection and deliver a credible response without the apparent erm's and in confidences. A telemarketer's best friend is a little black book that holds examples of their experience along with tried and tested rewritten revisions. The more you get used to writing your own, the easier it will come to respond in the live scenario.

The Warning Signs
Every conversation is littered with remnants of detail that warrant attention and scrutiny. Few of us can resist peppering our conversations with snippets of information that change the way we are viewed as people. If we knock the competition in our sales pitch it is easy to think that we are bolstering our cause, when in actual fact the opposite is often true. Each conversation we have is generating a picture of the type of company you are.

The reason I say this is because the more we open up and explore a prospects reality, the more chances you have of picking out the opinion from the fact. We need the fact to build accurate proposals and we rely on the opinion of the individual to develop a closing strategy, especially when more than one person is involved in the buying process.

Listen very carefully to the prospect when they speak. Don't get wrapped up in your internal thoughts about the situation or sit thinking about the next question you are going to ask, listen. You may be given a whole raft of useful information and you need to take control. Use open questions to gain the material and then slow down the conversation by saying "Let me get this straight" or "That's a lot of information, I need to write this down."

Let's look at a conversation and spot the warning sign and how to handle it.

Telemarketer: "So where do you see the company in the next five years?"

Prospect: "We have a bright future, lots of orders mean that we planning all of the time. I'd like us to open a factory in Belgium, expand our range of products and sell more of what we're good at. That's the intention of most of our board."

You see the conversation was really going well until the last part of the sentence. It would be so easy to let that comment go and be forgotten, but this could be the show stopper of the deal. At this point you have to ask more questions. What did he mean by "That's not the intention of all of our board?" It could be another opportunity, we'll never know if you don't question.

You'll also find prospects asking you for information and pricing even though they already seem happy with existing suppliers.   They might say "We've been buying carpets from Bradshaw's for over 20 years, send me your price list and I'll take a look." This comment may not be suspicious, so ask a few questions to understand their thinking. It wouldn't be unreasonable to ask "How many new vendors have you purchased from in that time?" or "What sort of conditions would need to exist for you to buy from my company?"

Price isn't always the biggest issue in a prospects reason to stay with an existing supplier. Family connections can often play a part, trading between both companies may exist, ownership by the same group, comfortable with the service, out of hours working that can be relied on to keep the customer happy, uncovering the sentiment will tell you whether you stand a chance of motivating change.

Another popular warning sign is "I will pass your information on to Mrs Smith." You may believe you have the decision maker, but this may not be the case.

"Does Mrs Smith make the decisions in this regard?"

"Will anyone else be involved in this decision?"

Handling the Objections
Do you fall apart when a prospect asks you about your value proposition? Do you feel aggrieved that the prospect has the audacity to question your approach or methods? How do you think it looks when your answer is less than rehearsed and confident?

At the end of the day we are all sales people. We are hurt when it doesn't go well and most of us do take awkward comments to heart. We are in this profession for the glory, to be the best and of course, to earn great commission.

In this section we are going to break down the process of handling objections, so that you can feel comfortable in your answers. Like most topics in sales you can prepare well ahead of time giving your conscious thinking the ability to react to all of the possibilities that get thrown your way. You'll react in a way that is thoughtful and sounds spontaneous.

Let's start with what is an objection?

An objection is an important communication that tells you that what you are saying is developing interest in the prospect, after all if someone wants to get you off the phone they don't ask you questions do they. If you develop the state of curiosity in the prospect they will want to know more. In their heads they are giving you a short amount of time to deliver a proposition and in return they need specific detail to see if it works for them.

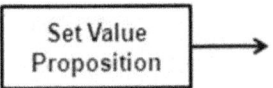

Set Value Proposition. Have a set, practised method of delivering your value proposition leaving the price until last. Work into your presentation over the phone, links to the needs the prospect has already given you. I say leave the price until last, for the simple reason that the price is irrelevant until the prospect can see what it will do for their company. If you say at the start for only £5,000 you can have our solution, then they will immediately think, too expensive. On the other hand if you say this product will reduce your monthly electricity bills by £2,000 a year and increase productivity by 5% every week, then all of a sudden £5,000 sounds like a great deal. Or even better for just £96 a week.

By following rule one, you'll be reducing the number of objections you are likely to get. Try and keep to the agenda as much as possible and don't let the customer pull you in too many directions. It's difficult to say what is the right amount of time to deliver the information and the answer depends on the prospect. If you deliver a three minute presentation and the prospect doesn't talk, you've gone too long. A good habit to get into, is to punctuate your presentation with questions, keep probing.

Telemarketer: "As you'll see the X500 is a wonderful kitchen gadget that a wide range of useful uses and doesn't have a large footprint on the kitchen worktop. Can I ask you a question Chris, who does most of the cooking in the house?"

Always pick a question that you can pitch a positive answer in both directions. In the previous example, let's say the prospect has indicated that they love to entertain in the house. The question "Who does the most of the cooking?" can easily be responded to positively. If Chris says "I do" you can lead with a context of benefits that aid him directly and how this unit will be appreciated by him or if they say "My partner" you can discuss how good kitchen gadgets make light work and allow both of you to spend more time on what's important, being with the guests. This is spin. You are essentially polishing the good aspects of your product to drive a build-up of positive emotions.

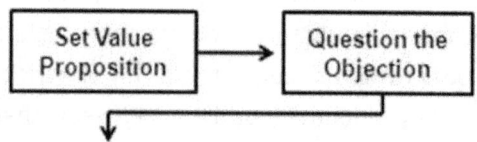

Question the objection. It is too late in the day to start assuming you know what the prospect is thinking. Clarify exactly what the objection is. For instance, the prospect might say:

"It all sounds too complicated for my business."

If you are selling a technology product you'll instantly recognise what I mean. Sometimes the technology is a great solution, but scares the prospect. Always reply with empathy and thoughtfulness.

"I see, what concerns do you have?"

Again the question isn't overly important, the empathy ("I see") and sentiment ("What concerns do you have?") however is. Get used to giving your full attention and just a few responses will get you by.

- "I can understand why (empathy), in such a short conversation these products sound complicated because they do so much (don't offer proof). Have complicated products been a problem for you in the past?" (understand the objection – listen carefully)

- "Has complexity caused issues before?" (hang on the answer, build curiosity)

- "Which part of the product do you feel is complicated?" (Break a big issue down into smaller chunks.)

Be inquisitive, the more you know, the easier it is to respond. When you listen, the picture you build up about the situation in your mind will change rapidly whilst the prospect is speaking. As you hear the words make small noises that show that you are listening like mm, mm, I see and do not under any circumstances try to give an answer to the objection early on. Even if the objection is an easy one to answer, take time and do it properly. If you answer all the easy objections quickly and a more difficult objection comes along which you have to take more time over it will be obvious to the prospect.

Try this out for size.

Prospect: "I like what you're saying and the principle of an electronic sea salt dispenser is a good one, but I've seen these devices before and the salt granules are too large to be dispensed."

Telemarketer: "Did you own a salt dispenser where this was a problem?"

Prospect: "No, we were at a dinner party and the host had just filled it up with new salt and we all commented on it."

Telemarketer: "I can see that the salt pot not dispensing at an important event could be pretty embarrassing. [Pause]

Can I ask, you said the host had just filled the salt cellar with new salt, could that have been the issue?"

Prospect: "I don't know."

Telemarketer: "It's such a simple thing salt, something we've all grown to take for granted. How many types of salt do you use?"

Prospect: "I suppose two, granular salt for the majority of cooking and sea salt for the table."

Telemarketer: "Good choices, and certainly ones you'd find most homes. You'll see when you watch the video online how these machines grind the salt perfectly and that's because…."

The example is completely fictitious, in real life I have no idea if there are different types of salt, but the words will be the same in every objection. Treat your prospect with respect and the understanding that they have no idea about the product or service that you are passionate about. In life we will all come into contact or hear something about a thing, a product or service and from that moment on we are building an opinion. At the end of the day, if what they hear in the first instance is absolutely outstanding then there will have little need for your call, the prospect would have bought it there and then. You are in the game of influencing the mind of the prospect to see value in what you are proposing.

In the example, the prospect has seen the salt cellar and around a table of say eight people the demonstration of its use did little to impress him, but it didn't go so far as to completely turn him off either, that's why he is still talking to you. The objection is simply him saying to you, convince me.

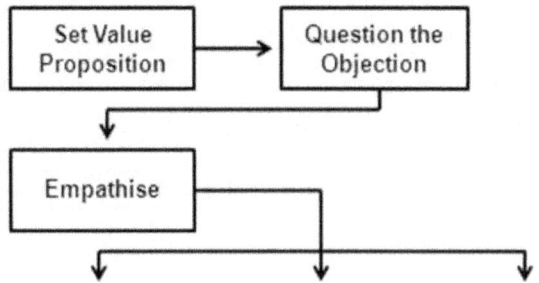

Empathise. You'll see in the previous example I used the line:

"I can see that the salt pot not dispensing at an important event could be pretty embarrassing...", this is empathy. Before you answer, take the seat of the prospect and look through their eyes. The question they ask holds some amount of emotional attachment. In this case the salt pot not working is hardly going to be a disaster in your eyes, although the prospect may have a different point of view. The prospect may believe that such a failure in front of people influential to their business could prove massively detrimental. If you find out you can at least empathise with the situation.

Empathy though is different to agreement. Do not mix your own social values with the point of view put forward by the prospect. You don't have to agree with a person's point of view to make a sale although you may choose to walk away from a sale if your own socially accepted boundary has been exceeded.

The prospect may say in response to your sales pitch providing an outdoor cooking utensil, "I don't think it's appropriate to sit outside and eat." This is a perfectly reasonable response in their eyes. It may not be your way of looking at the world, but this is not our concern. This prospect may have been bitten by a bee in Summer time and now prefers to eat inside. If your product is suitable for internal use, you will be able to handle this objection and make the sale.

However, such comments may break your socially acceptable code and you will find being empathetic impossible in the situation. You can always terminate the call. Don't be tempted to challenge the point of view. The conversation will turn into an argument and conflict will only raise your blood pressure. The upshot is you lose. Your attitude is now incongruent and you will find any further calls far more difficult to make.

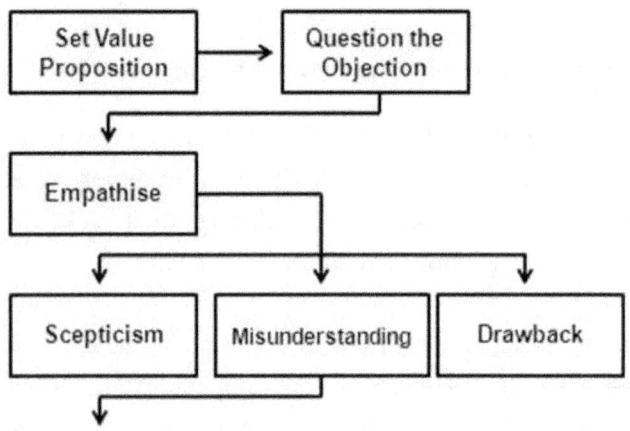

It is important to know that there are three types of objection, scepticism, a misunderstanding or complete drawback. All of these types need to be handled in different ways.

Scepticism. When a prospect is sceptical the message you are portraying about your product simply isn't hitting the mark. The prospects critical thinking is in the way. You'll often hear them make the almost inaudible sound of humming after you deliver your value proposition. In their mind, they can hear the words "I'm not sure about this, something isn't quite right." They are sceptical about the benefits that you are putting forward as a person. They may believe the reality of the product falls short of the value proposition you are making.

The answer is proof. Provide information that supports your claims. Now that you have a good understanding of where the objection has come from and you have delivered empathy, you can begin to provide a solution to the situation. You can do this verbally by articulating a crafted response or if the user is connected to email or the internet, introduce information that they can look at while you continue the conversation.

When you take their objection seriously you are asking the prospect to open their minds to some new information which they will be willing to listen to. If it appears that you haven't listened or that the information you are giving doesn't support the requirements of the objection then you are essentially turning the person off to your buying signals. From that moment on, everything you say will be seen with even more scepticism and the deal is lost.

An objection is yet another thing that you can prepare up front before the calls. Have a library of them. Write down the question, script a response and look at all the ways you can offer proof.

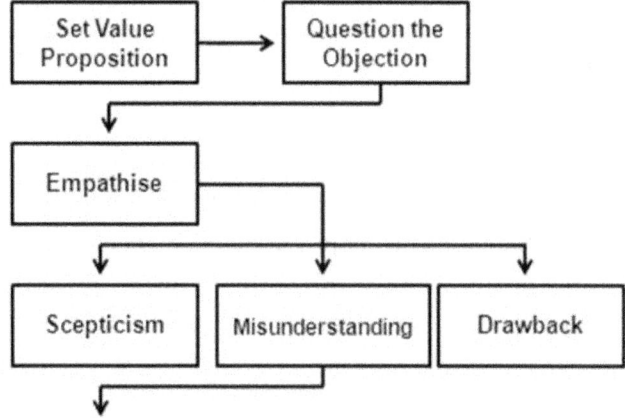

Misunderstanding. A misunderstanding occurs when a piece of information you have delivered is misconstrued when it is interpreted by the prospect. Remember earlier in the book we discussed how the speed we think, strongly relates to the speed we talk. Also remember that most presentations take a prospect from knowing nothing at all about a product or service to being an expert in a short period of time. The conscious mind can only process between 5 or 9 pieces of information at a time before becoming overloaded. So as you speak, they begin to stack the value of your proposal in their mind and begin to think of all the ways they can see them using your service. Of course, even though the information you have given was presented in a professional way and at the right speed, it can often be lost or misunderstood.

How do we resolve a misunderstanding?

We have to restate the facts. In your eyes the facts have always been accurate, now you have to reiterate the appropriate meaning of them. It is so easy to storm into a response saying "No, you heard me all wrong." This does little to build the relationship. Let the customer speak and fully understand their point of view before you say anything.

- "I can see why you would think that."
- "I hear what you're saying."
- "Let me offer some clarity."

These are all phrases that soften the language and these and other similar words can be used just before you deliver you restate the facts.

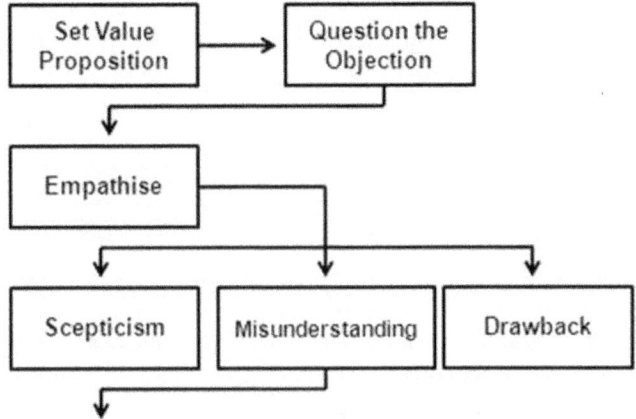

Drawback. Finally, the drawback. A question directed at a part or whole of your value proposition that cannot be resolved or changed. For instance, you may be selling cars and the one you have on offer is black and the prospect, only buys red cars. I am not saying there isn't a solution to this or a workaround. At some point in your presentation you will need to deliver an element of bad news in the value proposition to remain in a moral position regarding the sale. What I mean by this is, don't tell lies. A customer that buys and finds out they you have miss-sold is never going to be good for your business. This is where most telemarketers fall apart. They believe the words "I can't do that" will instantly stop the sale.

At first viewing the drawback seems more complicated, but really it isn't if you know your product and have listened carefully. Drawbacks are created by the prospect looking at the minute detail of your value proposition and not standing back to understand the whole picture. The context and background of the requirement are needed before you can answer, take this scenario.

- You sell fleet cars

- This deal is worth 10 cars over the next month

- You can deliver the model of car required in the right timescale, the customer likes this

- The XL specification has a better sound system and 2 more brake horse power

- The drawback is, that one of the cars is a lower specification than the others

You can see the dilemma, you have delivered the news that nine of the cars will be XL's, the tenth will be X specification. The prospect has recoiled with "I'm not sure that is going to work for me because I'd like my sales people to all to have the same model."

It sounds like a showstopper and that's exactly what a drawback is unless you can over come it. First of all, never assume that your solution to the prospects problem is riddled with holes and the competitors is perfect. Life isn't like that. Your competitors will have issues and problems as well, never second guess, but in this scenario it may be that they cannot deliver all of the cars on time or that the price is slightly more expensive than yours. The prospects job is to weigh up the pro's and con's of both solutions.

As usual, find out more first. Are all of the sales people the same standard? Are they all located in the same area of the country? I'd be interested to know, does it really matter that much?

Now recap on your proposition. The longer you talk the better position you will be in and importantly, step away from the detail. Speak more about the benefits of your solution than the one specific drawback.

Telemarketer: "I can see you like the idea of everyone having the same model of car, that's fair isn't it. But first I want to revisit the deal I have for you. The cars will all be delivered by the required date, I'll have them commissioned, cleaned and delivered directly to each sales person at a price, as I'm sure you'll agree is outstanding on these models. With one model at a lower specification, do you think that this solution will work for you?"

Delivery is everything, be confident. Give your answer with an air of "Why wouldn't you, this is a great deal" without being arrogant. When you understand the vision of the business, where they are going, how much are they spending, what revenues and profits are expected you can link your answer to it, delivering the bigger picture.

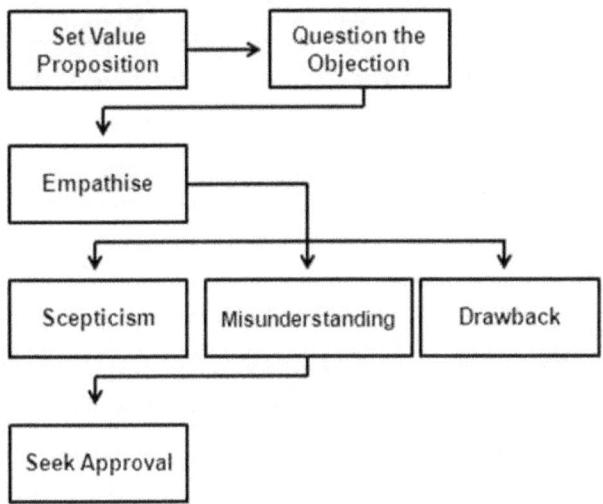

Seek Approval. You will have worked hard as a telemarketer to answer an objection, don't just wash over the subject by moving on without a response, ask the prospect if they are happy with the answer. I can tell you that you may say a lot on the phone, but the unanswered or weak objection response is the one thing that the prospect will remember. Tag your response with small questions.

- "Are you okay with that?"

- "Does that seem appropriate?"

- "Does that answer your question?"

If the answer is no, re-question. Understand why. This is your last chance to clear the objection. If they say yes, move on with your next part of the value proposition.

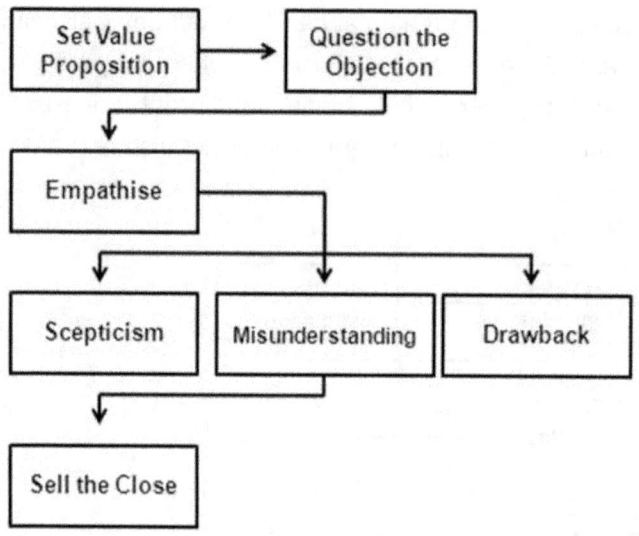

Sell the Close. The following transcript is a conversation between a telemarketer working for a paint supplies company and a distributor in the same marketplace.

Telemarketer: "As you'll see we have a wide range of paint products for both interior partitioning and exterior surfaces. We extend a guarantee across the product range, valid for 30 days which means that you never need to worry about defective product and offer next day delivery, to you or the customer ensuring that even tight deadlines are met."

(A small amount of example text showing that the telemarketer is developing a picture of features, advantages and benefits)

Prospect: "I'm looking at the colour chart on the internet and I'm not sure my customers will be able to use something on the internet reliably to get the colour they want."

(The words I'm not sure tell you that the prospect is sceptical about this element)

Telemarketer: "I see, is this a problem you've had before?"

(Always ask more questions, get to the bottom of why)

Prospect: "We used to sell products from a printed colour chart from Europe and constantly had customers returning them because the colours were so far off."

Telemarketer: "Yes, I can see that would quickly sour your relationship with them. (Empathy) Did you lose any specific customers?"

(Another probing question)

Prospect: "We must have lost a few, at least one of my good customers now splits his orders with a competitor because of it."

(In this answer you have developed pain, or the effect or consequence on the business. When you speak about the price of the product, be sure to have this argument in your return on investment wording)

Telemarketer: "I can assure you we have no such problems, we have the printed colour charts and you're right they are only good as a guide. We also supply small pots of actual paint so that your customers can see it on the wall. If you are on the web site now, click the pot button on the home page."

(Proof, the prospect was on the web site anyway)

"Do you think that will work for you?"

(Seek approval before you move on)

Prospect: "It looks good, but I'm worried about the extra cost. Margins are always tight in my game."

(I've treated this statement as a misunderstanding. I have not mentioned the price of these in this text, but it is stated on the web site)

Telemarketer: "Is cost something your customers speak about?"

(Probing question)

Prospect: "Not always, but sometimes I do get played off with competitors pricing, I want to ensure I offer the best value overall."

Telemarketer: "I always look for value, at least this small paint pot idea will help differentiate your proposals. (Empathy) The nice thing is, the pots are charged when purchased and the cost redeemed when they buy the larger tins."

(Solution and the benefit to the customer without costing the distributor anything)

"Will your customers have a problem with that?"

(Seeking approval)

Prospect: "Seeing on the web site how much they cost, I wouldn't think so."

Telemarketer: "That almost concludes my presentation, is there anything else you'd like to know?"

(Conversational summary, beginning to round up the presentation in time for the closing question)

Prospect: "I have one concern that as a company you aren't very local to me. I mean, I get lots of emergencies, hotels often want to run in and order and update rooms while the rooms aren't booked."

(A drawback, the company is 200 miles away and you cannot open an office near the prospect. – Paint a bigger picture)

Telemarketer: "How often do you get these emergencies?"

(Probing question)

Prospect: "At least once a month, we pull the stops out for people, it makes us a human and very user friendly."

Telemarketer: "Selling the service is a great way to stay ahead of the competition and I applaud you for it. I think what we offer as a company is a super service and we respond in the same way. I have some very experienced staff that are able to offer information whilst you are still with the client, the product has won countless awards and our reference database of happy distributors shows how much we care." (A list of benefits)

"We'll despatch our recommendations that same afternoon, do you think we can convince your customers together that this product is worth waiting for?"

Prospect: [Pause] "We might at least trial the arrangement."

(If there is a pause before they answer, this is good. Sit and listen. You are at the closing stages – well done)

Negotiating to close the deal

Your product or service needs to be sold at an agreed price and at times you will undoubtedly be pressured to discount to ease the sale. Again, the ideas we discuss in this section apply whether you are an owner operator or an employed professional. Define the rules before you speak to the prospect because decisions made on-the-fly invariably lead to costly mistakes. More money is lost in a second at this stage of the sale than any other. The promise of the order lights up our neurology to such an extent that the prospect can feel the time is right to ask for a discount.

In an earlier chapter we discussed how you should set your ultimate selling price. I am now asking you to be clear and set the price that you are not willing to accept, the walk-away point. The walk-away point is just that, it is a price demanded by the prospect that is simply uneconomical or unsustainable and it is your decision to decline the offer and refuse to trade.

This sounds a bit drastic doesn't it? Having done all of the hard work selling the benefits of your solution you then tell the prospect that you don't want his business. Doing business at all costs is a poor strategy. Think very carefully before you enter the realm of the loss leader, selling something lower than cost on the odd chance that you might pick up business later on, speculation is not a clever strategy in today's economy.

So now you have two prices, the RRP, recommended retail price and the walk-away point. Depending on the type of product you have this could mean pennies or thousands of pounds, so we need to develop a strategy to negotiate to close the deal with the objective of giving as little money away as possible. Negotiation as a subject is vast and it would be unrealistic to suggest we can cover every angle in this short text, but the following topics will broaden your knowledge and allow for a more efficient closing call. We'll take a look at:

- The importance of deadlines and compelling events
- Trading rather than giving
- Popular telemarketing negotiation gambits

Deadlines and compelling events. Your biggest ally at this point in the sale is the knowledge of a compelling event or dead line that the prospect has to fulfil. There is no point asking questions that uncover this at the end of the sales process the prospect will inevitably be less comfortable to give information away now. Developing a solid questioning and needs analysis skill early on means that you have all of the information you need to close the sale when the time is right.

If you sell cars and you know that your current rental period is the end of August this year, then you know when they have to act. If you sell crochet kits to wholesale distribution for the arts and crafts market and the biggest trade fair for the product is in July, you know that the prospect has to act. Without a compelling event or deadline date you have to have a really intense need to buy or the prospect can and will do nothing now. Now, I don't know if you've ever had to forecast your turnover to a sales manager with this type of prospect list, but let me tell you it isn't easy. Trying to tell an expectant manager that this order is going to come in this month because you feel it will, does not show competence. A sales manager will never expect you to close every order, but at least the coming and going of definitive deadlines will shorten your pipeline accordingly.

At the start of the process, expose the prospects wants and needs:

- "I can see that you are passionate about garden furniture, what makes you want to replace it all now?"

- "Is there a deadline to get all of these replaced?"

- "How much time do we have before you need prices and the items on site?"

It's not difficult is it? A professional buyer is trained not to tell you anything that could be of use in the negotiation and a professional telemarketer is trained to ask as many useful questions as possible, does this sound familiar. If you find the decision maker guarded, why not ask their colleagues or the receptionist? Especially when you've made a few calls to the business, the receptionist will relax their critical thinking and speak openly. They don't have an axe to grind and are generally very open and helpful.

Trading rather than giving. Next, get in the habit of getting something in return when you are asked for something. It is easy for a buyer to say "I want it cheaper" or "your competitor is a lot cheaper than you" and at the end of the day you may need to drop your price to get the deal that's appropriate. Tradeables are things that you can offer that have a high value to the prospect and lower value to you. Let's look at a few examples:

Time. You can offer an element of free time to get the work done. Be careful though, I am not saying discount your day rates or you will be held to this discount for the rest of your life.   I am saying a one off agreement to counter balance a requested discount. You may be a decorator and have been asked to wallpaper a lounge, when it comes to it they ask for a discount as the competitor is cheaper, you say:

"I would like the business and I have been exceptionally fair with the price, it would help me if I can show my work to two new customers this month, I'm sure I could accommodate your request if you were to make this possible."

Think of the home owner's position, they want a discount. You have been fair and asked for something in return.   Now they have a dilemma, a cheaper price or two viewings that not everyone would want to accommodate.   By instantly giving money away you are saying that your price was too high in the first place. Put pressure on the situation by taking your time. Remember, you have already calculated your walk-away point and are going to stick to it. This is one of the reasons you must always portray your business as busy. Never let anyone know that things are tight or you will end up working for nothing.

If you offer time as a discount always ensure there is an end date.

"This offer is valid for thirty days."

A free or discounted gift. We all like something for free. Two for one. Buy one, get the second half price. If they agree and you process an order on the phone, you even have the chance to up sell the product or additional consumables.

Change the specification. If they want a discount refer to an earlier version. For the money they are willing to pay, the lower spec'd model will do the trick and all they will lose is each of the following features.

Popular negotiation gambits. The way a prospect and a sales person influence the playing field of sales is by using negotiation gambits. These gambits are tried and tested methods of manipulating the emotion of the other person. If you understand how they work, you can adjust your response accordingly, remaining calm and unaffected. Here are some of the popular ones.

Meet me half way or split the difference. This is a scary phrase. When someone says this to you, you can't help but think how fair they are being in the process. In fact when you deliver the words "Tell you what, split the difference and let's remain friends" and they hold their hand out, you feel a compulsive handshake coming on. Now, that could be a good thing. You could be arguing about a few pounds at the end of the negotiation and this phrase, closes the deal in a brilliant and professional way.

The truth is, the meet me halfway gambit is responsible for more lost profit than any other negotiating tool. Take the scenario, your price is £1,000 and the prospect has been cheeky and offered you £500. With such a gap and it doesn't matter if those figures are larger, £1million to £500,000 or smaller the reality is still the same. If you set a fair and competitive price at £1,000 by giving a discount of 50% you are doing yourself a disservice and will look as if you are making inflated profits to the prospect. If you accept this offer you will have capitulated and given away a massive amount in one go, this is a not a good move. If the prospect says "Meet me halfway" you give away £250 in one hit, which is a great deal for the prospect. You response should always be small. Try responding with:

- Appreciate the prospects point of view
- Restate your value
- Make a smaller offer of goodwill
- Close

"I can see that our competitors are offering some exceptional price that I am unable to compete with, but what I can say is that the work I do is always guaranteed, we only use the best quality of materials that can be retouched as need be and I have lots of happy customers in the area that would be happy to recommend. I have a window of opportunity in my diary in two weeks, if you take that slot I'd happy to offer the cost of the undercoat."

My friends will buy from you too. How many times have I been made that promise? The prospect is saying, give me a discount and I will get all the other people I know to buy from you as well. Guess what it never happens. The moment they have their discount that's it, they forget you and the promise and walk away with a tidy sum of money. The thing to remember is retrospective discounting.

"I'm really glad you would recommend me to your friends because I know we'll do a great job. I'm always happy to offer incentives to people that recommend me and my organisation, after all its free advertising and word of mouth customers always pay quicker. This is how I work. I offer 5% of the value of the job in vouchers or cash for each new site I complete that means it won't be long before your work is completely free."

At the end of the day don't give money away speculatively. When you get paid by referred customers, its good practise to reinvest in your referrers, it hasn't cost you anything.

Take it or leave it. You will find some people try to apply pressure and say things like "That's my final offer" or "I can't do any better than that." The take it or leave it gambit closes the door on the relationship and should be used sparingly. Knowing your walk-away point is vital in making this work. The phrase should always be spoken with empathy and reflect that the price quoted was a far deal and the current discounted rate is as far as you can go. You may want to leave the call and say, perhaps if a slot comes up later in the year you may be able to oblige at a later date, although this current surge of trade isn't likely to stop anytime soon.

Summary – The Professional World of Telemarketing

You have embarked on a career that holds untold riches for those that approach the industry with professionalism. Like any other art form, telemarketing is a combination of personality and technique working together to influence the buying populous to share their wealth with you. It is an ideal opportunity for bright and exceptional minds to excel in commerce and other aspects of business life. No matter which direction a professional telemarketer eventually takes, the skills learned in this book alone will propel them into even greater success.

Learn on the job and review this text regularly. Prepare well and reap the rewards. The life of a professional telemarketer is within your grasps.

www.ingramcontent.com/pod-product-compliance
Lightning Source LLC
Chambersburg PA
CBHW051713170526
45167CB00002B/646